DISCIPLINE *n. v.*

# DISCIPLINE N.V.

A Lyric Dictionary

## CONCETTA PRINCIPE

Palimpsest Press
1171 Eastlawn Ave.
Windsor, Ontario, N8S 3J1
www.palimpsestpress.ca

Printed and bound in Canada
Cover design and book typography by Ellie Hastings
Edited by Jim Johnstone

Palimpsest Press would like to thank the Canada Council for the Arts
and the Ontario Arts Council for their support of our publishing
program. We also acknowledge the assistance of the Government of
Ontario through the Ontario Book Publishing Tax Credit.

Canada

LIBRARY AND ARCHIVES CANADA CATALOGUING IN PUBLICATION

TITLE: Discipline n.v. : a lyric dictionary / Concetta Principe.
NAMES: Principe, Concetta, author.
IDENTIFIERS: Canadiana (print) 20230157882
            Canadiana (ebook) 20230161642

ISBN 9781990293498 (SOFTCOVER)
ISBN 9781990293504 (EPUB)
SUBJECTS: LCGFT: ESSAYS.
CLASSIFICATION: LCC PS8581.R5512 D57 2023 | DDC C814/.54—DC23

*I dedicate this book to Phil Phil,
my beautiful feral, who read with me and watched over me
with love and caring, and still does from where she is (may she
rest in peace) through all my struggles; this book is for all those
who watch over and care for those who struggle.*

# TABLE OF CONTENTS

"If the history of thought could remain the locus of uninterrupted continuities, if it could endlessly forge connections that no analysis could undo without abstraction, if it could weave, around everything that men [sic] say and do, obscure syntheses that anticipate for him, prepare him, and lead him endlessly towards his future, it would provide a privileged shelter for the sovereignty of consciousness."

— Michel Foucault, *Archaeology of Knowledge*

# FOREWORD

The pages ahead tell a story of the collapse of the Ivory Tower. What happened? Or better, when did it happen? In truth, I have very few answers, but in 2014, when I graduated with a Doctor of Philosophy, I was deep inside it, this animal of knowledge, and could feel the weakening of her bones, or was it her heart? I'll tell you, I witnessed, unknowingly enabled, and was the victim of how the corporatization of the academy was dismantling her, discipline by disciplinary piece.

What is it? That sound? Standing there, on the second floor of a building that I have walked through day in and day out; that generations have walked through day in and day out; those days *ad nauseum* during which the sun infiltrated to little effect, east to west, a dull knife of ozone, day in day out. Ghosts maybe? Gothic tales were born here. Or just the crux of her foundations. Or maybe that's Martha's eternal fail?

Passages. Bodies through passages of a tower as if the tower should never change, except to slump at the corners, or curl up at the edges, as photographs do. The ivory tower as photo album; or as a body with its arteries and administrative heart pumping. Bodies inside this Body, the Arche of thought, come and go; and then there are the bodies that pass through and get spit out unceremoniously. Bodies that self-harm. Bodies that have sex or toke in the washrooms or meet for clandestine exchanges in classroom corners, after dark. Bodies that come back and co-opt a corner office. Just as this body of thought is having a seizure. A 'stroke.' A thought strikes me. Past tense of stroke is 'strike.' In the second month of my PhD, we members of the union of sessional workers *went on strike*.

I tell my story of passing through those halls and in my 'passing' I have sometimes passed out from the anxiety of passing through. In passing through these halls, I have tried to discipline my body to keep breathing so I won't pass out but will pass; I note that disciplining the body to breathe, mind over body, is a fallacy; efficiency in the time of no time. Excellence. Where is the excellence?

In the pages ahead you will hear my unconscious speak through the discipline of study, passing between anxiety and lucidity; between salad, niçoise or otherwise, of all messages infiltrating at the same time, overwhelming the body, the mind unable to sift and digest, which slows everything down to sludge. Breathing problems. Metabolic effort. Contrasted by days when I can see light years away.

Anxiety as the cause of anxiety (teleology), which means that messages just filter in and out, light through windows, without any chance of being sorted out as meaning for the mind. You can't put your head between your knees because you're in public; to show any weakness makes you unfit for the job market. I am trying to fit: fitness in the academy, calisthenics of being chosen. Anxiety. Breathing problems, my billowing, bellowing chest a manifestation of some deeper secret, a pearl under the couch of my depression.

I am, some days, quite lucid. I can see for miles. From the second floor of the tower I can see at the end of the hall, beyond the door under the EXIT sign, bright red. An accident or opportunity? Climb the stairs to the fifth floor to that corner office stripped of all its books for the professor on sabbatical. There, rows and rows of teak shelves, suspended on those metal arms braced by a bar against the wall, bookless, becomes my office one year, a lucky break for a sessional to have the best corner, ever: south-west. Not a dull 'closet' of space, with no light or working chair. Toronto at my knees covered in light and lake Ontario at my toes. Sitting at a desk in front of my union-wrested laptop, working. I did not have a smart phone then, so that meant leaving or listening to voice messages only. Hooking in to eudorum. All articulating the elements of lucidity that comes after you have 'righted' the wrong of your body's unconscious desire to kill itself. Or is it the death wish? Drive.

I am so driven.

Looking up from my desk, I can see the edge of everything, clear, irrefutable, and so fine I lean in, I marvel, I touch... dehiscence. Disassembling. Straining for focus, splitting occurs until breathing problems return, with all their semantic trouble. Really hard to know the 'cause', 'cause trauma returns in the best disguises and clauses. Closets. Offices. Orifices.

Through which I have passed at every stage, the learning experience reflecting the crumbling institution itself. Some trouble at its foundations. At mine. The fifth-floor shakes periodically. Was it the literal shudder of a city or the shudder of meaning in my head? Yes, the Ivory Tower in convulsions, capitalism killing it slowly, salt spread on its roots.

Back to the thesis that twitches in the shuddering. The thesis...

Maybe this crisis is not about poisoned roots. It could very well have to do with removing the bone on which knowledge has been built, returning each part to its original place of rest. Colonizing as a canalizing of life, as per the wisdom of Marlene Norbese Philip. *Zong!*

I am a body inside a body, between the Charybdis of syntax struggling for oxygen and the Scylla of lucid dreams, polarities joined by the amniotic fluid of logic. There's shuddering ahead, in this archive of Ivory Towers. Please bear with me and enjoy the passage. I am where you will be (*Wo Es war, sol Ich werden*), in the dust of a body enduring an earthquake.

We are at the twilight of white privilege and all her boney corsets. No wonder I can't breathe, Godard.

I watched it come down, this tower. I was one of the people who participated by not doing anything... not quite a part of the party. This is a memoir of academia and how white its hallways. Until I came and all that white crumbled. Do I give myself too much credit in making possible Equality, Diversity, Inclusivity and Decolonization? What am I capable of doing? With my disabilities, not much other than make it through. This is a memoir of ability and failing to be able. A memoir of Becket's failure in my mouth: fail again, try again, and fail better...

# FAILURE

My failure does not start in the third year of my undergrad, first year at U of T, in my second year class on Chaucer. But I will start there since it's relevant to my degree, my suffering (we all suffer), and the reason my application to the PhD program in English Literature at York University was rejected. It was a shock, rejection always is. I begged The Chair for an explanation. He was a medievalist, someone whose scholarship was on Arthurian Legend, who had probably aced Chaucer, so he was embarrassed for me when he explained my D in Chaucer "didn't impress the committee." That impression, in fact, led them to reject my application.

My doctoral degree started with a medieval failure.

My Chaucerian prof at U of T was affiliated with High Anglican Trinity College, the oldest and most prestigious college at the university. She was so High Anglican that she talked that way: chin lifted, trans-continental. Yes, she spoke the imperialist accent. I don't think she used regular toilet paper. I don't know if anyone liked her — she was old and of a different order. None of us were equal to her. Her bones were brittle, which is why she loped in with a cane and a broken hip on that first day of class. She was gracious after all: goodness, she had so much grace, much in the way a New England snob does. Almost a masonic, closed and very suspicious of foreigners. I was suspicious, in name and colour. I was the dago born of working class jeans, destined to be a salesclerk at Cotton Ginny.

Apparently, Chaucer said "K-nigh-t" as the Germans did. She loved to say it, all its consonants sticking as they rolled along her teeth and tongue.

I had also read Joyce's *Ulysses* that third year of my undergrad, thanking god I'd read Homer's *Odyssey*, and loving Joyce's Penelope. For the first time, I read *Sir Gawain and the Green Knight*. K-nigh-t. A tale I would reread too many times to count.

The volatility of my personal relationship at the time, the anxiety of being abandoned, the anxiety of not knowing the future, the terror that I was destined to fail…

I failed my first assignment on Chaucer. In fact, the professor said that day she returned the essays, "if you have failed this assignment, I advise you to quit, now, while you're ahead." I couldn't. Why? Because I only give up if I'm thrown off the boat. I didn't drop out and was refused boarding to the doctorial ship because of my D, or disease. Or was it D+? A matter of a degree.

With the Disavowal of a King who is about to lose his kingdom, I turned from the 'letter' that said 'no' to my PhD application in English, and applied for an MA in the Humanities Program where I was accepted. I saw no significant difference between English Lit and Humanities. And unknowingly, I had become affiliated with all the MA MA's in the world: the double Master.

# WHY? — A WORKING THESIS QUESTION

Why would I walk straight into failure? Why wasn't I smart enough to accept NO and walk away? That's right. Why would I do something that was going to hurt me? Why wouldn't I listen to my body? Why wouldn't I heed my disordered thoughts? Why do any of us do things that hurt us?

# LOST AND FOUND

**DISCIPLINE 1:** I entered an inter-disciplinary graduate program in Humanities because the English Department rejected me. I had only a vague sense of disciplines, but no real knowledge of how a group of disciplines could define what is called "The Humanities;" that humanities disciplines are not those disciplines found in sociology; that the former is traditional, per se, and the latter rises up from new soft-sciences; that the study of biblical literature in the humanities is textual, and not at all related to the science of archaeology, which is sociology along with anthropology; that at the institution where I was studying, humanities often wars with sociology, because it is the 'other' multi-disciplinary field and needs to maintain its funding. Though a smaller division, humanities' power is rooted in the traditions of philosophy, history, political science, languages (though not the social science of linguistics), and of course, English Literature. Until my PhD, it had never occurred to me to see English as one kind of fruit of the humanities project, nor to consider how constructed disciplines are; it explains why people outside of English speaking communities can ask, when I say I studied English: "Oh you studied languages?" No, the literature. How does language signify multiple cultural artifacts? I crammed my mouth with all this disciplinary jargon, jamming the porcs, the hair, nose and eyes, not quite seeing how I was manufacturing a hole.

**TTC TRANSFERS:** Not all holes are obvious. And those we fall into rarely announce themselves. After that first event, or accident, we circle the hole abstractly, distractedly. For example, long ago this wonderful woman I knew who was smart and could read anything, laughed this one day when she saw me pulling TTC transfers out of my jacket pockets looking for a matchbook. "What are those?" she said. I smiled, embarrassed. "Just TTC transfers." "I know," she said, as if her question was rhetorical. "It never amazes me how people live their metaphors." I looked at her confused. That confusion lasted for years until I recognized the metaphor she saw. It was the bridge, you might say, over the hole that was my TTC. And that hole I can date to the winter of grade 2, when my box of many words was taken by the dragon of the TTC. My shoe-box was filled with many many words I had learned up to then: I had so many things to cart around, this being winter with the boots and the coat and mittens. When I arrived at school without my shoe-box, my teacher demanded: "What happened?" "I lost my words," I said. "What do you mean you lost them?" She exclaimed in front of the class. "I lost my language on the subway." I didn't actually lose it: rather, I forgot it. But it's truer to say that the dragon ate my words and no Lost and Found would bring them back to me. My paper transfers the transference of how much it hurt to appease Pluto (Poseidon) and his hunger.

ARCHAEOLOGY is a soft science of holes fathered by Heinrich Schliemann, a rich German businessman in the nineteenth century who had this fantasy he would find evidence that the war Homer represented in his long poem, *The Illiad,* was not fiction. It was history. I learned about Schliemann when working on a television documentary series on biblical archaeology. He was looking for the bones of the Trojan horse. He was looking for a comb of Helen's beauty. He was a punch line in the editing room, where I would sit with the editor, as we tried to parse the scenes of the episode so it made sense, trying to make the holes look good. The joke about Schliemann was that he was a squirrel, looking for his winter nuts, except instead of digging, he planted them. That way he established the methods of archaeology, the discipline of it, in negative terms: all his methods were the methods any animal with instinct wouldn't waste their time with; the methods a human being wouldn't admit to using, for ethical reasons.

**PSYCHOANALYSIS:** Archaeology is as old as psycho-analysis. So, not very old. The science of lost causes of the psychic life. Odysseus had Poseidon terrors trying to get home from the wars to Penelope. He fell into katabasis and met Tiresias, the blind. Dante's tortuous screwing down to the last abysmal layer of hell. Dig me a cake, Betty, seven layers of it. Deep into my belly. Dear Herman Schliemann is digging it — the semantics of the subway's dark continent. Little red riding hood and her box of letters. "Better to scare you with," said Schliemann. Literature and ethics. The unethical bastard salted his 'troughs,' became a laughing stock. Best soft loss: my glasses on a beach somewhere in Italy, circa age 5. Walking with holes in my face. Best hard fall?

**SQUIRED YOU:** I am standing by the doors to Cotton Ginny, when my Chaucer professor walks in, dripping with New England treasures. Chaucering her way around the cotton racks, dead for centuries. That didn't stop her from k-nygh-ting me with near fail, over peach-puke sweatshirts: "oh, how retail becomes you!" TTC again. Word falls with winter, thick slabs of it under the tread of summer-camp shoppers. And with that, my Chaucerian k-nygh-t walked out with the flash of a gold tooth that laughs, "Squired you". Red cheeks running to the toilet. A howl through the porcelain fixtures, that maybe everyone and no one heard. Here, even here, the spluttering of Monty Python's horse-less knight. "Put up your dukes" to thin air. "Take that." I'll cut off my right arm to prove courage. I'll cut off my left arm to make my point. Here, I'm sawing my eye-teeth for the k-nife word.

## SCHLIEMANN INVENTOR OF BAD METHOD:

To prove Homer's famous piece of fiction was historical, Schliemann went digging. He dug troughs and when he found nothing, he filled them back up like a good boy cleaning the mess in his room before starting another trough. He dug and dug. He dug here and he dug there. He dug troughs everywhere. And when he paused in his work, he couldn't say where he had dug and where he hadn't. He started digging where he thought he hadn't. He kept digging. He wouldn't stop digging and could afford it, which is the first discovery of most archaeologists; you need money to support what appears to be a useless cause. You could say: he dug circles around himself. And when he was fed up with not finding anything, he threw something in the pit: this is called 'salting' the dig. Then he found things that were unnamed, anything things in the ground, and named them. That piece of gold he found he called Agamemnon's mask, which led him to exclaim "I have gazed upon the face of Agememnon!" Betty's glasses are still buried near Rome, should Schliemann be interested in Agamemnon's eyes. But her words,

**NOT ARCHAEOLOGY:** Schliemann was retrospectively judged a hack. His work was judged as what not to do. For one, Schliemann just landed in a field and dug, a squirrel searching for nuts. Unlike Schliemann, the serious archaeologist chooses a field on recommendation and when the dig starts, must keep a daily record of where 'he' [sic] digs: keep a precise record of each trench opened and document what is found there, even if it is nothing but a few cigarette butts. This is the principle of provenance: proof that what was found was found 'in situ.' And when that 'trough' has been assessed, the serious archaeologist can fill the hole, assured that 'he' [sic] has carried out a successful operation. The foothills of Judea, watch your footing, foot in your mouth. Footprints everywhere, footnotes abound. The books prove it.

**ARCHAEOLOGY OF THE MIND:** Sigmund Freud, the father of psychoanalysis, was fascinated with archaeology. On his death, he had 2000 artifacts. Archaeology was a science that he saw as parallel to the methods that may be used in psychoanalytic treatment: talking through, a digging into the metaphorical significance of dreams to find the 'artifact' that lies hidden, holding the jewel of a subject's being. That jewel, we must acknowledge, is not the beautiful thing, but in psychoanalytic terms, is the alien artifact that human consciousness must hide at all costs. The seed of compulsive behaviour. The grain of sand in an oyster's shell. This 'pearl' in Freud's science was the psychic wound that he named "trauma," after the Greek word for wound. And in completely archaeological terms, the 'site' is identified by compulsive behaviour: the unconscious 'spits out,' unwillingly, an artifact much as buried things are 'revealed' when earth is moved by deep seismic upheaval. Bones in a box. What happened here?

**BONES:** I rediscovered academia via the backdoor to the basement. I, Betty, sat and waited, smelling as shallow as TV documentary. Yes, the plumbing is a problem in the Roman toilets all over Judea. Masada had bakers and a postal service (pigeons) and that archaeologist who claimed the naked truth was, in fact, naked. Tracing carbon-14 threads on oven ash, every tortured Judean accounted for by a stick, or is this bone? Every plot twisting on a racist Herod, circumcising things right down to the fine print, every talking head marking time under the ancient sun. Betty waits patiently in the basement of the ROM for bad news. The Carbon testing of that bone they found on Masada was not ancient human bone: "bird not man," the doctor said. "Sure, maybe pigeon," when Betty asked. "But not ancient," the doctor adds. This tantalizing taste of heuristic method. Message received. Meanwhile deep deep down, between the desert's legs, the dead sea salt; where did it start, the idea that discovery had meaning? That discovery was not on television, but in the hallowed halls of intellectual study. It started in the subway, word, platform no podium, foot and mouth, returning to work not even noticing all that cannibalizing with impunity. Missing why Agamemnon's face kept sliding off.

**KATABASIS #1:** I had a special relationship to biblical archaeology. For one, I had been reading ancient Greek literature for years. Well and truly, I knew Homer's *Illiad* like the back of my hand; but Odysseus, that was palm reading. I'd read James Joyce's interpretation, and after that, Dante's *Inferno* (katabasis). I couldn't bring myself to his paradise. And between them, I read the poetry of the anti-Semite fascist, Ezra Pound. I discovered the landscape of his Pisan poems — "Zeus lies in Ceres' bosom" — those he wrote while imprisoned for treason in an American POW camp near Pisa, using a typewriter on a box, and a chair that a guard had snuck in for him. "do'an you tell no one I made this for you." He told everyone, and everyone loved this guard so much that Pound looked far less ugly, at least while he was suffering in prison. The guard, something like Tiresias, blind but fair, who gave the lonely Odyssean what he needed to survive eternity.

DISCIPLINE 2: The discipline of English literature was the 'ground' of the interdisciplinary work of my humanities degree, but was not my first choice. The discipline of media studies, film and television, was an obvious choice, but this scholarship did not turn me on. Having worked in the industry, I saw that it was a shallow California beach; everything was surface, everyone bounced their beach balls, everyone regurgitated what others said, lounging by the pool playing with their towels or bikinis; everyone was asked to be chipper, to be catchy and dumb-it-down; that was my task as a researcher-writer-director for a TV documentary series on biblical studies and archaeology. Soft science bouncing in the waves, I handed deboned fish to the star of the show to cook up as it suited his naked knees; did he go around in shorts? I can't recall now. I learned a lot and everything I learned stayed with me. The discipline of "English" was not my first choice, it was my default, my first steps, my first words. Biblical studies followed me into the hallowed halls of authentic thinkers.... Or I was the follower of its crumbs, or maybe more like a squirrel, chasing nuts.

**TO CHASE:** To chase meaning down the hill, to chase the bone all around the yard, to chase and dream and fall flat in the ditch. I knew how to chase, having worked as a chase producer: I chased scholars to invite them to get in front of the camera and talk with the 'naked archaeologist,' this wild and fearless host of 'arckhaios + ologia' (ancient history). Fearlessly he waded into Israel-Palestine unafraid of being seen as a Zionist, unafraid of bombs. He waded into the debates between secular and sectarian historians, and laughed. He believed there was a Moses; he believed in the message from The Mount. He believed that there was a mass suicide on Masada, that great palace Herod built for himself, which became the refuge for the Sicarii, what historian Josephus claimed were terrorists. So explains the Josephus scholar on camera. I left the shallow waters of film and television for academic depth. I turned my back on that path for a future that suited me. And who should I find in the very program I entered because of my failures? It was the same biblical archaeology scholar. In hindsight, the first indication that I was chasing failure.

**OLD MAN AT THE SEA:** She came to the sea of PhD, and the old man there. Even now she doesn't remember much of those first years: there was a sea and dusk fell through the halls. Katabasis, my Tiresias, she thought. The old man. Could he see what I mean? What did he say? She came to the sea and asked him a question and his answer was "Know." She came to the door and even when he opened it, his answer was "Know." She came to him and said, "Listen, this is my thesis: will you work with me?" Drive around and think about it. What did he say? Did he say "Know" as in the Kantean "Dare to know!" Was he as cryptic as that? She drove around it many more times in the night, in her sleep, in her dreams, for days and months. It took some years before she heard it. The "No." Circling an empty net. Circling because nothing was straight and playing at history is a defensive mystery.

# WRITING THE DISASTER

"Withdrawal and no explanation. Such would be art, in the manner of the God of Isaac Louria, who creates solely by excluding himself."

— *The Writing of the Disaster*

**WRITING STRIKES:** We were on the front lines in the resistance against capitalism that was sucking the blood of academia. A disaster, what capitalism facilitated. The strike answered with its own disaster: after five months on the line, unemployed, we were returned to work like bad kids by Premier Wynne. This is how I began my PhD. And I saw the disasters compounding. Much as the CBC divested itself of producing documentaries by outsourcing its budget to production companies at reduced, freelance wages, so the academy was turning us all into freelance professors. It was a joke that was hard to laugh at.

**THE FIRING SQUAD:** Strike reading: Maurice Blanchot. A French resistance fighter in WWII, he wrote *Writing of the Disaster* about the experience. Ostensibly about the Holocaust and the death camps, in truth, it was a confession, in the Augustinian sense. He talks about standing among many in front of a firing squad, waiting for his death, and waiting... but Blanchot survived because the death squad abandoned their post. Or did he survive because he converted from fascism to resisting Hitler? Because he crossed the floor. Blanchot accepted his fate under Hilter's regime, waited to be dead for doing the right thing. Waited like a good resistance fighter. But it didn't happen and when he realized this, when he and the others around him understood, his first thought was that he was immortal. He lived through his own death. His living is a kind of parable: do the right thing, fight for humankind, and you will be rewarded with eternity. Isn't this what Paul of Tarsus said? Follow your heart in Jesus and you will rise from your mortal coil to be rewarded with eternal life?

**THE UNIVERSITY ASSETS:** The death squad of my defence: the scholars who bought their homes with income made off of artifacts lifted from native soil and the forced migration of those artifacts into museums, archives, homes for the Lost and Found. M. NourbeSe Philip talks to Livingstone. The spreading of biblical history across museums and universities in the west. The movement of human labour as slave trafficking. Return my people, Africa says. Give me back my language, the Anishinaabe demand. Some are found and the rest lost. Pluto haunts every move. How am I supposed to see right from wrong if I need to jump hoops to come out the other side to get a job?

**ETERNITY:** I can see all around the face of time. Borders of hours brimming rimless, spinning Blanchot as beyond human. Body immortal. A sea of forever. Compared to the scholar who accounts for every minute of his life defending a territory he colonized and will relinquish over his dead body. Tenure vs. Maurice Blanchot on disaster. The firing squad visible through the black hood of my thesis defence. To be hooded. Wait. Wait and work. Anticipate the riddle of bullets. Wait, what happened? Right, nothing. The men with guns lined up in front of the bodies with hoods and then disappeared. You see them, you see them not. Seeing nothing, the prisoners wait, standing at attention, heads bent toward eternity.

**THE PICKET LINE:** From here I saw the future. That we would be a long time on the line. I was right: we were called back to work five months later, broken, broke and angry. I also foresaw a tenure-less future. The writing was on all our faces, on the picket line, colleagues fighting for a living wage. I foresaw my freelance future. Capitalism, a boring machine, turning us into swiss cheese for the sandwich they serve in the caf. But I had the privilege of King-thinking, could turn from the writing on the wall: disavow the future running ahead of me.

**HOLE AGAIN:** I blame my failures on the fact that I fed Pluto all those years ago. It is so hard to turn away, turn it down, change your mind, especially if you aren't forced by a war to see your crimes, as Blanchot was. Everything begins with a hole, says Lacan. I bide my time through my degree, waiting for this hole to do something.

**ANOTHER ETERNITY:** Holes do nothing. Anorexia is nothing. It is the 'lack' at the centre of lack; it is the satisfaction with. Nothing. Forever. It is the negating of nothing, holing all. In this hole I hold some eternity, a piece of apple. It has no tomorrow. It has been covered in shellac like those restaurants that display their rice, shellacked; it satisfies the anorexic every time they pass, seeing the inedibility at the heart of all things. They fill this heart with books. They eat the words, which taste good. They devour Lacan who fills a vase with the negative space of his thinking, a kind of water for the mind, a 'thing' into which one may add fish, paper shellacked broccoli, or green apples. Watch Lacan's water circle what is not. *Une pipe.* Drawing space before the cat wakes.

**WASHING WITH DIRT:** Doubling back: the letter of education, the level of dedication, the bevel of seduction, in the suds, in the wash, the wear and tear of deduction. By her want of what he wants when she cannot read his mind. Waiting. By her weighing the law without organs, he wants crackers to go *snap*. He wants you to attack, or at least learn how to be a man. Or at least compete decibel-wise with that guy who spent the whole class trading on the stock market. The women all mostly silent. Nothing compares to the *jouissance* of tears scrimming—no, I mean screaming in your face. Red as sunset, scarlet of Pacino's rage, the alpha scar purloined by the fascist jerk. Hormones running free along the hills of Derrida's Marxist ghosts, stolen and spoken for, messianic. Thus spoke Zarathustra through the halls of this institution. And pigeons should be so lucky, washing with dirt. Breathe.

**SALTING:** Reading history between my days on the picket line. I was once a camera on Masada, facing pigeon holes, wandering across the stony palace, documenting the ghost of a bread event. Archival, elemental, wide-angle on individual mistakes, looking up to appreciate Herod's intention to protect himself with a stone palace he carved out of the mountain cliff, overlooking the dead sea to the east and leagues and leagues of desert to the west. Scholars and filmmakers milling about. Salome was here, John's head on a platter. Baptize that, seven veils for the seven layers of hell. "It's dark in here," she said. He whispered back: "I'd like to meet you in a dark place." Those were the words someone overheard at a shoot who heard 'meat.' Kincaid's baker and his bread. Dare I share that story in class? History and so Heidegger's worlding, that kneading of dirt and civilization, punching down what has risen. Social and political geology. So tempted to Schliemann my thought, salted with stories of being there, where the Sicarii died, finding the femur of one of Herod's pigeons. Or this thing, this is from Jesus's left foot. Not.

**ROTTED:** After continually working the picket-line, weathering a shift in season and the glares of both tenured and administrative employees, my favourite maroon lace-up leather boots were done. Rotted. Ruined. The salt had eaten between the toe and the sole. A petty but significant disaster.

**MASTER DISCOURSE:** From the very rims of her glasses. The cotton rims of her armpits. The rims of her written eyes. The drive is everything. Fuck desire. Fuck the washing. From this rim we wipe the glass holes and musicalize. Hang the washing and draw diagrams. Give me breath and break the blueprint. Sometimes violence is the only means of setting the bone. Rim of the bone on the eyes over which the woman with her coffee relishes your potatoes wishing not for artichokes but for those goddamn boots. Choking on the rim of the laces. Drive the car around the river the way we walked it in winter. With purple rims round blue rims round brown eyes. So rimmed in beige cotton that no one could imagine his eyes were blue. Not at all the unconscious resistance. A monster of revolution. The ladders of inception. The mothering one does out of necessity. The loving one wants to give for free but there's a cost for everything. Economy kills but is Marxism answering the door? A messiah complex was his crutch, his lash. The cycle of desire means focus. Over the edge of this bowl, staring deep into the void where it will begin. Hole this very thing.

**EMANCIPATION:** I remember we were in a hotel lobby watching the American election reporting that Barak Obama had become the first black American president. We were there to ratify or reject the latest contract. Our rejection of management's compromises coincided with America's modern Civil Rights movement.

**SATURDAY NIGHT:** Fed up, she breaks the seam of the book. Burst of starlings fed on wedding rice. Bust inside, under the pink cover, maroon and spineless now, brittle as flowers drained of summer floating up the river. It was *Twelfth Night* he pinned his promises with a wildflower. England in all those books. She breaks the fast-lane and Betty is driving again. Time beats and beats. Kierkegaard on repetition? Or Don Juan, sans Mozart, epigraphically, tea table and a chair, and annihilated. Beats me... Beating the board; beating the dress; beating the flower into a ghost on the stairs. Beating the odds at Woodbine. Beating. Beat beating. I bet that Betty was overjoyed with the dressing. Beating the horse is a crime in all countries. Beating the chest to say, "I did this!"

**HORMONAL EXCITEMENT:** Working on a PhD is not work; it is a digging into the binds of a historical tradition and that, apparently, is sexy; it is exploring the precedent, which is meant to get the boil going; it is listening to dead men talking while leaning in to your neighbour's breathing; it is not talking; it is talking all the time you are listening to the sexual energy spinning round the round table. That light. What is it? What is it about mental work that gets the hormones all fired up? To be told my hair was so 'voluminous', today, on this cold January, let down from a pony-tale. Embarrassed by being objectified, unearthed and even Victorianated, Dante's lovely Josephine. This is kindergarten, and I'm oblivious to what the kids are up to.

**THEORY:** Dionne Brand wastes so much time on relationship angst in *Theory*. I could care less about the gender of the talking I. Especially because the gendered I, trying to un-gender itself, uses the Master Discourse. As such, the voice castrates everything, without discrimination. Even without discipline. You see, in the institution where discipline reigns, where discourse is the Shibboleth, well, there is only one gender, it is the testosterone ink that takes the sexual organ for the act, veils the one who is all lack, because, really, "there is no sexual relation," as per Lacan.

**THE DIG:** I dug around in the muck of my thought and destroyed forests with the effort of digging. I ruined water with every bleached revision of a paragraph. I gave the paper mill a reason for being. I gave so much in my taking. I took so much I was devouring provincial parks with the fire of my words. The fires blaze; my mind on fire. I kept the paper mill in profits. At first I dug, much as Schliemann did. Not that I believed the Dead Sea Scrolls would give me Jesus. The exact opposite in fact: I was looking at history much as Freud looked at the history of Judaism in *Moses and Monotheism*: there were two Moseses, and the first one was killed: guilt for that murder returned in the sacrifice of Jesus, his absolution of the historical sins. Which no Christian would ever understand. Whereas Freud was trying to explain why Jews were being persecuted, I was looking for the archaeological trace of the relationship between anti-Semitism and the formation of Christianity.

**THE DEAD SEA SCROLLS:** Salt and script. Sewing my tongue to my lapel was an accident. Script and fault. Chewing my lip was a mistake. Sea and script. The sea will make you float. Skin scripted with salt and mud. The salted script. Salivate and you've salted the dig. The fragment known as the messianic fragment is so full of pompous self-aggrandizing bullshit it reeks even now of being a counterfeit. Yes, this is what I want to write about, the trauma of this. "What do you mean?" he said. "No, jesus wasn't there, no matter how hard they looked." Salt and mud. Stick in the mud. Not a bone of the saviour. Sodom and Gommorah. That's the sound of crust on crust. Bread and water in the desert. Lot's wife as a pillar. May I have an extension on the Dead Sea Scrolls? The salt of the earth. Azure and salt, t-bones on the grill, sun in the sky, skin in the game. Teaches you to look back never.

**WHAT IS IT?** What is it about academic work that as she digs, she goes nowhere? As she digs, she is whistling through the torture of what 'attracts' them. Attraction as traction, the kinetic force of attention. It is gaping, this action. Wound a heart, talking. I can see the lips spinning, the aorta mimicking rhythm: it's not all about sex, not at all. But sex is happening all over the place. Can you smell it? This is not the point. It's about that first disaster, that failure that you can't let go. Why is there so much repetition? It's so hard being under it again. So hard not to sink; tread or swim; swim and sink. What is it about the academy that takes your breath from out of your ribs: an eden of the mind, daring you to get back to it? You can't hide anything in here; but hide you must. Doan you let no one know.... What is it about the academy that no one is going to listen unless you dress it in the 'right' New England accent, have the right tone of testosterone? What is it about academic alchemy that brings out the priest's cloth and knives? You don't mind if I nip and tuck, do you? Shame is your dessert. Live with it.

**YOUR AGE:** The days can't be unstitched now. They are so close together, all those moments imbricated, one into each other, a fabric of suffocation. They say that panic attacks are the terror of dying. I guess this is killing me. Unlike Scheherazade who could add, I was subtracting, inch by year. Breathlessness indicates that someone is walking all over me: I am dead. How did I get here, Tiresias? Why am I so old? I don't feel any older than a ten year old. The roar of the disaster in my head. Stitching my reasons so that yes, it's hard to breathe: it's hard to say why I am so old at the age of ten. Alone in this field: it's okay. I've done it all my life, and I can do it some more. How did I get here? The analyst says nothing.

**THE MENTOR:** A woman who was doing her PhD in dance, whose artistic flare probably outpaces her critical skills, saw everything and told me what she saw. She applied to one of those fancy American critical theory summer courses, where a young scholar had the chance to work with such academic stars as Žižek, Butler, Derrida (who was not alive, remember) etc. She made it in. While there, she paired up with a friend doing his PhD in the US. He helped her with her writing: "This is terrible, A—" he said, she told me, her face cringing. "He wasn't gentle. But he said his mentors were the same." And then A— described what is likely the natural order of academia, which is that there are adoptions based on one's ability to be turned into the one who deserves to be chosen (mesiach/ messiah), leaving the rest of us just corn for the pigs. A—'s friend barely slept, revised and revised everything he wrote, and even that was massively rewritten by his mentors. He was being adopted for one future: TT at one of those leafy eastern campuses, such as Northwestern, Yale, Princeton, Cornell, etc..

**MINOR DISASTERS:** I'll never forget the fight between tenured profs at my weekly Monday night seminar. A disheveled unionist (who experienced an ethically black and white conversion to tenure track, after years of fighting the good fight as a CUPE) took up arms against my soon to be Master supervisor who was lecturing on Benjamin. My would-be supervisor was explaining to us that Benjamin understood translation owed a debt to the 'original' text. The translation translates 'truth,' the first cause: translation can only approximate. The postmodern anti-truth, anti-essentialist, anti-universalist, CUPE union fighter, slaughtered the Benjaminist with typical academic speak: playful verbal abuse. Slaughtered him in the way a union mog would slaughter management, with loud rhetoric to undermine the Benjaminist, who received the attack with all the grace of royalty and responded, soft-spoken, with some honest disdain and conceit. Still, you could you see he was a little shocked, a little crushed. Neither academic moved an inch, but the sparring was the fireworks of their graffiti tags in the evening air. Some bruising, but no blood. A disaster only in the minor sense.

**ACADEMIC STARDOM:** In the academy, #METOO caught up with NYU professor, Avital Ronnell, 66, a renowned scholar of German and comparative literature, who was accused of psychological abuse by one of her PhD mentees. Fifty intellectuals, including Judith Butler, defended her at trial, claiming her achievements were proof she crossed no ethical boundaries. Hailed as an "important figure in literary studies at New York University"—never mind. The list of reasons not to condemn her goes on, reinforcing this whole 'business' inside intellectual practice: the agents of production must be protected at all costs. So what if there's abuse? Abuse is a biproduct of academic production. Abuse happens. How do we do Marxism in houses ruled by a capitalism that sees no ethical virtue in addressing abuse? Hollywood or NYU: what's the difference? What would you say if I told you Avital was mentored by Derrida? The man who wrote about Marx's ghost. What is mentorship? Never mind.

**MY EXAMS:** I didn't add the Book of Job to my reading list. But I have never given up Job's dilemma. The one none of us can answer: why do good people suffer disaster?

**BOOK OF JOB:** There were jobs and there were no jobs. There were jobs, he said. Do I want a job in this place? There will be jobs, she said. There were no jobs before and I worked in the mines all those years. There will be jobs. The sun cuts the rim of her tooth. Blood breaks. There will be jobs. Suck it up. "I'll drive," she said. "Stop," we cried. The deer missed us and the tire rim flew into the sun. I notice, there are no jobs. Kierkegaard. There is no repetition. Deleuze. Everything is repetition. Exams next week beneath Rosenzweig's star. Jobs. The Book, I mean. I have loved you always and will never stop, Johannes says to Cordelia. Betty's love for that star of redemption (Rosenzweig, remember). Star, stella, Rosenzweig's disaster. There's no way they could fail her for loving him: that was a dream. Kierkegaard on memory and repetition. He says that is not true: there are jobs. Many jobs. Jobs that come rolling off the GM line about to shut down because Blanchot, the bird of eternity, lights heavily on the branch of universal daycare.

**THESIS #1:** Advice I understood so clearly when it was given. Not to me in particular, but to a group of PhD candidates in class. "Concentrate on something so infinitesimally small (the thumb and finger together barely two millimeters apart, which from this distance looks like nothing) that you cannot imagine how you can write even a paragraph about it. Believe me, you will be writing about it for decades." I didn't believe him.

**OLDER THAN AVERAGE:** The foundations of academia, foreign jewels and good history, are being dismantled, slowly. Postcolonial discourse becomes Diaspora discourse, which is now the project of decolonization. We are a colony, after all. We are de-toothing our archives. Shame on me. I should have come to the decolonizing campaign long before my academic peers, considering I am above the average age. An A+ for longevity, me and a sweet man who had to step down for health reasons. Can't teach an old dog new tricks, they say. A fallacy sure, but a maxim that sticks. I am I because the dog I don't have will be. Yes, a kind of erasure of older female students in the academy. Not out of malice, but out of shame for being; out of embarrassment; out of the Derrida aleph, a beginning before time began. What's she doing here? Maybe adding some jewels to her name. She doesn't bend enough, bow low enough, smile wide enough, and definitely speaks out of turn too much. Definitely not TT material.

**ANOTHER FAILURE OF A THESIS:** "Quit now," one advisor advised. To think I could just walk away from the firing squad of my defence. I thought long and hard on the edge of this. To quit as in, walk away, to leave, to stop smoking. We had a barrel of fire to warm our hands as the leather of my boots rotted with strike mandates. To fill this waiting with smoke signals. The rim of a void of nicotine signifying the latest flirtation. Smoke and mirrors. Blanchot, did you ever feel seduced by some Johannes, renamed his Cordelia? Eternity answers with apples falling in the idyllic grove beyond the cantilevered situation that has me dangling my badly shod left foot, reading this tome on Badiou's event while imagining I am at Frank Lloyd Wright's Fallingwater house. Left foot, right; left food, night. What is it? My bangs I did myself. They are my thesis, thanks.

**THE FUTURE IS DANTE'S HELL:** There are circles of hell here in the academy Betty will not see until it is far too late. The seven layers of an upside down cake. There are those who never enter, leaping over the void to be greeted by the Dean at Northwestern or U of T. There are those who precariously circle the mouth of hell, securing limited term contracts, year after year, contract after contract. One day they will be old and fall. There are the various levels of seniority at your institution, the lower you go, the more obscure their features. Miners of truth, their imaginary rising to the top, ghosts. And those of us at the bottom, walking the streets of this netherworld, unable to afford a coffee much less a beer. Not even an interview. Most of us are white. And old. And women. Various discriminatory euphemisms are used, but not aloud.

**TIRESIAS:** I came to the walls of this PhD with double vision. History and Literature. Marx against capitalism. The old bard named Homer. What's in a name? What is history? What did he say? He answered, "No" and a hole opened beneath my feet. My Katabasis, I should not be afraid. I came to the door of Homer's Tiresias and asked, "Listen, what do you think?" Meanwhile, down the hall, Marx was gesticulating, a slight of hand so no one could hear capital working, 24-7, or notice the cracks widening. After all, you take out a corner stone, and things up slide down, vice versa. Obama was president, but was that a great thing, if civil rights could be trumped by a white supremacist? The white halls being woked during my tenure as a PhD.

# PLATO'S CAVE AND THE GOOD NEIGHBOUR

*"Much food stored in a Cool Cave"*

**ANTIPHOLOSOPHY:** Lacan does not want to answer the question: who am I? Knowing that "I" is not 'who' but "what": split inside, awkward once the spectre of Oedipus enters the room. Sort of what Plato means by the cave. And Socrates and the logic of human thought. But then there is Parmenides, which is Lacan's reflection on Plato's dialogue... but I run around Plato here, straight to the scraps, the fragments of the ancient philosopher, Parmenides. What he said was: what is is, and what isn't, isn't. If you can think it, even if it is not, it is and so will be. That's a thesis.

**OLD MACDONALD HAD A FARM:** My son and I are on the front porch, doing little. I'm reading. We see a man eating a Big Mac come down the narrow path between our house and the neighbour to the south. Maybe five minutes pass, and two more men, one tall and the other short, holding McDonald's drinks follow the first guy. A girl and two guys, also McDonald's, bag and drinks, slip between our houses. It's a Sunday afternoon. Is there a party next door, I wonder? Another guy on his phone, a smoke, no McDonald's. Two guys come from between our houses, cross our lawn in the direction of McDonald's. One arrives from the south. Two guys meet in front of the neighbour's house, no McDonald's. They stand there, idling, exchanging notes. Two guys arrive very fast, cut across our yard and disappear in the gap between our houses. They had McDonald's my son said, standing at the window, looking at them. About five people leaving the neighbour's house cut across our lawn, the traffic is too much, maybe McDonald's. "I want a happy meal," my five year old says. And then for a long time there is nothing. My son and I on the porch again, he's happy playing with his McDonald's toy, waiting for the sunset. The cops arrive, two sedans, walk between our houses to the neighbour's basement door, and when they reappear, our neighbour is with them, hands behind his back. We have just moved to this neighbourhood. According to our neighbour across the street, we are living next to a crack house. Or, you could say, a crack basement.

**WEDDING HALLS:** This house was once beautiful. I could feel it in her bones. So I replaced ugly doorknobs with glass doorknobs: I put baubles all over, and even painted over wallpaper in the second floor hallway. There was a pattern to it that made it look like the lace of a wedding dress. I named it the wedding hall. I baked Betty Crocker cakes to teach my son how to bake cakes and called myself Betty. My son loved it when I played.

**THE CAVE:** My son's first fire is a candled pumpkin monster. The shadows on the wall are different. *Differance.* I am reading and I can't get the shapes straight. Unfair and tame as the whip cream on Betty's pan-whipped short cake. I cannot. How to make cake while reading anti-philosophy? Eat my crumbs, he said. No, he didn't, that's a joke. The neighbour is in his cave. Now bags of McDonald's in a stream of visitors' arms, cutting across our lawn to visit our neighbour's katabasis. Repetition. "No," says Deleuze. "Don't waste your time," says Plato. He will go out and just come back again.

**PhD, YEAR TWO:** Myself and rimmed; the dim light of the edge of the glass; wine brimming with music. Dark nights and fascists. Smoking and smoked salmon. Salamander. The fire is running out. Bike, bus, foot. Footfall. Always falling. The fall is a bad time for me. Bad timing.

**STANDARD GRADUATE CONFUSION:** Initially, I had no idea what Derrida meant. Foucault's *Archaeology of Knowledge* confused me too. And then Freud. I understood Freud a little since he's essentially mechanical. The human body, for Freud, is plumbing: the mind all that cathect, the electric of the light-switch, electronics and cathexis. Saussure. That's when something in my head clicked. Saussure says: the tree outside your window is not the word 'tree' that you read and speak. *L'arbre* is the French word for the English word, tree. The word is arbitrary. I felt like that doll with big black dull eyes that suddenly, in a blink, has deep and peering vision. This was followed soon after by a colleague who stood in the freezing cold smoking, while explaining: "But Foucault's so simple. He's basically saying every new discipline has stolen words from the discipline it grew from, then made new words with those stolen words." Is this the cannibalizing of culture; the violence of words; the colonization of the mind? Then back to Derrida. It's when you look at the binary of night and day in Jacques is/isn't, that you see the pair is this function of definition: one defines the other. A word is defined by what it is not. When you pull this binery wider, Derrida says, you see how that space shows you that the preference for day over night is cultural, which means that the preference is not natural, and in that sense, in the sense of logic, arbitrary. Nothing natural about 'stone.' Ah, but what a word.

**BREATHLESS:** The archive, as Derrida highlights, speaks to the future. Bread crumbs in the cave, socks on the floor, as if I knew one day I'd be on the short end, outside, filling with a tide of anguish. It's Sunday, and we're washing again. His favourite socks had starbursts on them. Looking back, the spinning inside was not about the scholarly machine: it was about looking up from the failure of my degree to see that what was good had long gone. The look in my son's eyes. Anguish erupting at discovering the loss of a pair of beautiful socks. Looking back, there was never logic to my breathlessness. Panic attacks. The time, the narrow gate of 'seconds' that I opened for two feral cats. My lungs are pore-less. My blood is lightheaded. I hear the stars are bad in here. I let my eyes roam back to the cave, by the fence where my son's beloved Silver broke her neck. And every Sunday, without fail, another dryer of countless divorced socks. The dryer is a cyclops. I try as hard as I can to hide my grief from him. So I joke, at least it didn't take your foot.

**PSYCHOANALYTIC COUCH:** Lacan and the pass. Does she pass muster? The mustard with 'hot dog.' The dog is not hot enough, my son said. Lacan, pass me the salt, will you. The dog of Lacan's Freudean debt, dogged, full of faith. Jesus's parable of the mustard plant. The dog needs to take a walk. "Jesus," the walking mustard said. The hot of Lacan's tongue. Pass the bread, I'm starving. The hunger of Lacan's mustard. Jesus was here and left. What did he say? Jesus wept. Lacan repeated himself, unwillingly. The dog of all that is passable. Dog days of summer. Lacan has stopped. Jesus was. It is August.

**FAILURE:** I told a scholar that I wanted to explore the 'messiah' in current political and cultural projects. His first response was that this was a terrible idea for academic scholarship, that maybe I should just transfer to divinity school. When I wrote an essay on the Christian origins of secularism the scholar turned on me and said "this is a secular institution and your religion does not belong here." He told me that I might be better suited to keep my focus on biblical studies, as no one today wants to hear about religion since God is dead. Nietzsche killed him. Didn't you hear? I didn't say that Lacan brought God back out of necessity. Another scholar who was not my advisor also advised me to take "religion" out of the equation. Words like 'saviour' would be better, was the suggestion. I bristled: 'saviour' is Christian, not the a-sectarian principle that Derrida-Balibar-Benjamin are reflecting on which is the Hebrew 'mesiach' or messiah. A third scholar told me she was interested in this study on Jesus and I panicked: no, not Jesus, though he was considered a 'mesiach' by his Jewish followers of the time. Derrida meant something else. I wanted to understand why Derrida wanted us to think that a messiah comes back in a secular world, not as Christian or Jew or even Muslim, and that, for Derrida, is okay. The professor admitted Derrida confused her.

**THE CON-CAVE:** Zarathustra. Zarathustra. "God is dead." Nietzsche kills it. He's done it and there is nothing left to do. Lacaned you.

**PLATO'S CAVE:** The cops again, talking to the neighbour, and now everything is quiet. This vale of universal tears will water the garden, bring back the crust of grass from the dead. Everton pines for Trinidad in Toronto streets. An Orpheus, the grass his Eurydice. Versatility. Verse or poesie. His room-mate took off, he said, leaving him with a flooded basement and mould. I don't say that the nosey neighbours and the cops always target black men as crack heads. Minding his own business it was the roommate who was dealing. What's the thesis? Catholic. That won't do: too sectarian in our secular age. Versus the way that Betty circled winter on the lake last summer. So singular. So never to be repeated, that elliptical motion. Thesis on the philosophy of history.

**THE CAVE OF MY DREAM LIFE:** It is Derrida. It is not Derrida. It is a dream of Derrida. It is not a dream. It is the book of Derrida I read, in a dream. It is Derrida and it is not Derrida. There is no difference, really. Derrida in my dream is Derrida who is dead. The spectre of him. For him, I suppose, his spectre was Marx. It is a dream to meet you, I say to Derrida. I say nothing to Derrida. He smiles, and he doesn't. In my dream, this is not a dream, and he is gracious. The living Derrida is not alive but in my dream he is what he was when alive, grace of a beautiful mind. I believe this. I could have said that, when she asked me, "What do you believe?" I believe in Derrida and I don't believe. I believe he is dead, but really, he can't be if he comes to me in dreams. Can he?

**COLONIZATION:** Trinidad, Everton said. That's where oranges grow full and sweet in the sun. He sings to the grass in the dark. It's my mom's song, he says. It's beautiful, I say. And he smiles, shyly. He has been abandoned by his roommate, not a friend, he said. He's been made to foot the bill for rent. He's the one who went to jail for all the crack that was sold. Wasn't him, he swears to us. It wasn't him. He just hung out there because that's where he lived and he couldn't do anything about it.

**BREATHLESS #3:** I am lying in bed in the dark listening to a man sing his mother's song to the grass to fall asleep. In my dream I am sitting with everyone, and Rosenzweig, my master and my love, is there. I am asking him for guidance. I am asking him, what happened that night he decided not to convert to Christianity, as was his plan? The star of his redemption; the light of his thought. I am in the place full of life that begins with death. At the end, there is a wonderful moment of countenance, a sun radiant in my mind. The power of redemption is only light. I have been so steeped in it, so saturated with Rosenzweig's being, that when I come to the garden and the gate, I realize he is letting me go. "Live," he says. "Stop this meandering in here and go live." So when at the first of two exams (in my dream) I am asked a question that is not about how much I love Rosenzweig, I cannot answer it. I am faced with the knowledge that I will fail. Do you want to know what really happened? A question was posed and I took the discussion in a direction I preferred, if I recall correctly. And while talking, I had this horrible feeling that my dream was coming true. Later, when I pass I exclaim, "I had a dream about this and was sick with the fear you would fail me: but I knew you couldn't possibly fail me over something as petty as..." They look at me and lower their eyes. The face of failure. To this day, I believe I only passed by the skin of my chiny chin chin.

**WHAT ARE YOU AFRAID OF?:** Deep in the vault of who we are, says Plato, is this wish to retreat so we don't know what we've discovered. Plato's cave and my son's joy. We spent hours creating dragons, vultures, and tyrannosauruses with our hands in the shadows on the wall. Shadow puppets are a joy, an ironic binding to the parable of the cave. We grow into the cave of our ignorance, reading the shadows on the wall, in joyful terror assuming those massive movements are of a being that, should we move, will find us. Odysseus hiding from the cyclops. Sure, even if a shadow has one eye, it has one that can easily be blinded, as per Odysseus. In any case, the chains that keep us caved and shrinking in terror from those massive things about to get us are merely the restraints of our anxiety. Breathe in. Count to five and breathe out. My son admitted to waking in the night too terrified of Mars invaders to scream. One of us ventures out. I guess it's not me. No, I'm telling Plato's story: maybe he was the one who snuck past the raging demons, and, on looking back, discovered the fire had cast illusions of demons on the wall. In one flash, the monsters vanished as clouds will when winds come. The wind of freedom, of vision. But try as we might, we do not stay out here. No, says Plato, we will we go back to our beds made beneath the spectres of terror and will remember freedom as a dream, an illusion, compared to this dark cave, so solid and so real. Freud and Lacan stand next to Plato here: yes, what causes terror are mere illusions; but terror is so real we can't believe we could ever live without it. What do you believe?

**IN THE CAMERA:** Trauma can be understood as the flash of the bulb of a camera. That flash erases vision for a moment. What happens, exactly? The 'subject' of the shot is still there, but they've changed. The photograph is there to prove it. Sontag and the pain of capture. The soul, they said, caught by the punctum. That is the 'stain' on our retina when nothing can be taken back. The soul cut open, an orange, and beheld by the tain: that silver coated surface wounded. We call it etched. I am thinking in particular of Carson's wonderfully impossible photograph of the fly, captured in a 15-minute exposure, "floating in a pail of water." Death animated as "a strange agitation of light around the wings." The aura of life. Geryon is such a great photographer of trauma. Geryon is not Carson. A fact we have to keep reminding ourselves, as scholars; the fact we have to remind students as they read; the fact that 'subjectivity' can and should be troubled since, yes, the author is not the writer; the narrator is not the author; the character is not the author. I am not writing this: Betty is.

**A LITERARY THESIS:** The garage is listing right and the landlord doesn't care if his tenant gets sick due to mould. Human rights? The law is clear, and the police can enter if they deem it is unsafe. "Who has the right to tell me what I can do?" demands the landlord. Meanwhile, the good neighbour who sings to the grasses accepts the Nile of his dwelling. With his mother, he brought our grass back to life. After all was said and done, the right turn was the wrong one, he said, telling the truth. But that didn't stop him from feeding his mother's songs to the night, the worms, those lying in their beds with the window slightly open. And my son would run with cans, tuna or beans, for him, that his father had given him saying "don't tell him who is giving it to him." Doan you tell no one I made this for you. A thesis of the bad left foot.

**THESIS, ORIGINAL:** There is only one thesis into which every other part of anything falls and it is haunted. It leapt out at her one Montreal night where too many ghosts wandered in and wouldn't stop talking. What is it? Your thesis, I mean. What is it? Well, if it is, then it is; it if isn't, it isn't, unless you can imagine it, in which case, it is. That's Parmenides, not me.

ATTEMPTS: ????????????????????????????
????????????????????????????????????????
???... Each of those indicates a 'draft' of the first attempts at saying what I mean. Looking for the wave to lead me past the demons binding me to the cave.

**THE POINT:** A good thesis is one that is a sentence long and ties everything together. A good thesis says everything the way a basket circles the point of its being. Its essence, you might say. It presents the space for which the fruit, nuts and bolts, bread, or messianic aspirations, are to settle. A good thesis is sunlight through the woven grass. What is, is. What is not, will be, if you can imagine it. What is it? Something that interests you.

**SALTED:** Swimming the semester while the prime minister pontificates. Do not eat the bikini. I'm talking Sponge Bob as a piñata. Shimmer. Grim reaper in the rhyming trim-work of his new home, which meant he wasn't paying attention to what was happening in Crimea, where his wife was eating shrimps. Write another paper. Provenance. In the dead sea you will never drown. The wound of her thinking, all over the place, digging at the vein of a broken mind. Maybe go back and start with an outline. Too many lost causes. A basement that has a Nile in one corner, always rising with the flood. The scabs shimmering in the bowl of Eden's forbidden tenderloin, aleph of my heart, artichokes and clover. Salad again. Who gives a fuck? Swimming with the crimped bangs of a rough winter. Betty confesses. I did them myself, she says; they taste alright. All by myself.

THE *MUSELMANN:* Remnants of Auschwitz. I need to be simple here. To explain why I have a thing about the messianic. Why it relates to Blanchot and it doesn't: because Blanchot sees the disaster of Auschwitz. Because the hell of the camps was not just in the machine that killed, because many, including Kaufman's father, provoked their own death as an act of faith, rather than have it stolen in unconscious starvation; the hell of the camps was not even theft of what the inmates were forced to part with, or the theft that Spiegelman's father's retelling shows us, as the means to get what will keep you alive. It was being turned. Turned into a Nazi enabler for those extra shards of bread; turned into a tool for spying on comrades to stay alive; turned from your father, as Eli Wiesel confesses in his *Night*. Turned inside out of context, reduced, cut apart, and reconstituted as *Muselmann*. The word which, as Primo Levi observed, indicated the ultimate shame of 'submission': the spark of humanity past being an ember in the husk of a ghost of a man (*If this is a Man*), the one who cannot see one's submission, but is seen by those, such as Levi, who are afraid of becoming that, and therein fill themselves with shame, as if to save themselves from being shameless. In this weave of what was, will be, not at all, and horror, a messianic remnant is woven, binding our witnessing to that false turning. The retrospective privilege of prayer. As if Blanchot is shamed in not having been forced to submit in the camps, he confesses his disaster as nothing; as if he might have been *Muselmann*, at the mercy of the Nazi engine, if the Nazis had forgotten his fascist alliance making him no one. That he saved no one, but as no one, still exercised his "weak messianic power" against fascism.

**STELLAR:** The pattern of salvation that we inherit comes from Paul, and still works, perhaps because his starlight is practically the same as our starlight, even though he did not see the sky as we know it now. Kepler, a seventeenth-century scientist, questioned the theory that stars circled in perfect orbital spheres, never colliding, because they are inside clear glass baubles keeping them at a distance. Inside baubles as if hung from heaven's floor. Kepler thought it was bunk, this baubles theory: his theory was that stars moved freely in perfect elliptical orbits because they were sentient, had free will. A natural perfect tango, contra Lacan's claim that there is no sexual rapport. Today we know stars do not collide because they have their own gravitational center. Unlike humans who get tangled in their need for sexual rapport, stars have no need for intimacy with each other. But what could Kepler know, having only Tycho Brahe's impressive lists of degrees of starlight, documented over a lifetime: a kind of manual labour of the camera punctum initiating the empiricist method? Small secrets of the universe have come from wilder theories.

# WHAT IS HISTORY.

"it raises an object — and I don't mind the suggestion of the play on words in the term I use — to the dignity of the Thing."

– Lacan, *The Ethics of Psychoanalysis*

FERAL: I was reading for history the January that a feral tabby walked into the hallway from the frigid outside, and turned to enter the living room where she threw herself on the carpet. There was a bit of melodrama in that 'throw.' There was a slight shock in every move she made. She had never ventured into the house this far. She had never entered the house from the front door either. I think she let out a tiny cry when she fell. She swooned — unusual drama for a feral tabby. I bent down very slowly, careful of her wildness, cooing to her in squirrel sounds, and reached out my hand to scratch under her ear. Took her ear with thumb and finger and felt the burning. Fever.

**WHAT IS HISTORY?** It teaches us nothing. Logically speaking, history is not a subject. It cannot say "I," nor is it internally broken by itself, as the Oedipal subject. Not even Paul of Tarsus who saw himself as both "I" and Jesus; both dead and reborn. My *méconnaissance* of life as dead. They say history is what you make it, though history claims there is only one truth. So what is truth? Can we even handle the truth? Deductive reasoning here: history does not need to teach to be considered a subject.

**MESSIANIC COMPLEX:** The vet said I saved the cat's life: she would have died from the infection of the wound, a deep slash vertically down her skin that just missed cutting into her trachea. Her healing involved staying in my office for the whole winter. Saviour is a complex.

**THE CONCEPT OF HISTORY:** What did you believe, Benjamin? He believed, maybe, that the angel of history could see the 'true' past. The rubble of the crisis smoldering in the distance. Still smoldering for me, here, far into the future of that first vision of the angelic power of vision. I am throwing Derrida as a part of lacy smoke on it all. A veil. Derrida's Archive Fever is about this very moment that only the angel has access to: it stinks. It smoulders. It's everywhere in the air and has landed on my taste buds, slipped to the back of my throat. What is it, this sticking? The stink makes me cough. I feel sick. Fever. I am burning with it. It smolders for me, because of me. The angel is my dog with ears to hear through time. The arrogance of every writer, right here, in these fingers writing this, wagging her tail. Messianic as a fever.

**IS HISTORY SEXY?** History is a soft art, one that pleasures the economy of rhetoric. The science of gender butters Latin and Greek, sexuated, declining—or is that reclining on the bread? There is nothing to learn from history, the historian said, citing by not sighting Kierkegaard's theory on repetition hanging on the wall. Foucault in his back pocket, unseen and creased. The rim of that room, with the windows circling questions thin as the tain. He declines Greek which renders History speechless. This would suggest history speaks.

**QUIET, PLEASE:** They talked. She talked. No one talked. Odysseus can't talk, remember? He's a character. The streets talk of bad feet. The boy wouldn't talk, no matter how hard the torture. They all talked. The room talked. The talking was a sound around the graduate study hall. No talking please. They talked anyway. They all talked, talked, talked. *The hours spent with my nose in a book except the day I had to stand in the bus, my arm hanging from the pole hiking my shirt revealing skin, the guy in the chair below me, not reading his book, looking up at my skin and swallowing and I thought about all the different hungers.* Ok, let's whisper. They talked in a whisper. They whispered about Paris. Schliemann couldn't take it anymore. They talked about that. Remembered to whisper, "I told you so." Stop it, you're driving me crazy. They talked about uptight people and gathered their books and left the graduate lounge still talking. Then in the silence, he started talking.

**TALKING HEADS:** Sorters and dividers, seers and peers, agents of change and movers and shakers doing radical shit. Interdisciplinary study is a promissory note, this heady milky way of discussants, dead and alive and yet to be born. Intra-disciplines of say History and English, borders deeply entrenched, staunched by a fear of bleeding. This water-colour anxiety. In the off hours, they love to hop the fence into each other's backyards, dandelions and salamander not-with-standing, pretending there is no envy of each. Monday morning, though, History is back stressing there is no fiction in it; and English will tell you that philosophy is not literature. And Philosophy will concede to the possibility that theory is a branch of it, but if you haven't read Hegel you can't read Derrida, and literature is for wimps. Derrida says anything is literature. Foucault says history is man-made. Saussure introduces the wild-card of arbitrary signage. No wonder there is theory anxiety in certain corners of the academy.

**DISCIPLINE 3:** When I went wandering the halls, building my committee, some of them smiled watching me try to scale their publishing history; when I arrived, they got upset for wasting their time. No hand to pull you up, no comrade in arms, not in the 'corner' of thought where I was standing, at least. So, I went alone out into the fields, disciplines in singularity; me jumping walls of tumbled divisions, scaling sheer and terrifying texts. I had that English Lit rope, after all, and could do pretty amazing things with it, such as crossing borders to mine fallacious arguments; oh my joy of close reading, or sucking the semantic marrows dry. With discourse, I wrote my name over other names and did so with a singular perspective, one which no one except, perhaps, God or Carson's Geryon, could read. If they even bothered to look. Or were interested. I brought my committee from three fields. I roped them to my cause. They sat separated by their different '*langues*,' and no matter how hard I worked, I could not bring these three together for me. This you see, is my close reading of my PhD.

**WHAT IS IT:** I missed it, the circling around the fault in the argument: to *langue* the room and no one bites. The racoon clawed this close to cutting through her trachea. Anus, mouth, nose, ears, what is history but each foreclosure of the throat. Arche came with set theory. Make me laugh to set this theory as a bag. A condom of sorts. A sack of potatoes, all tied up tight. It was impressive how this material historian could speak Foucault, which was not his science. Pleased with himself pleased her more. Deep deep down she could feel it in him. To think that anyone can have a hidden rim that was so visible... her very lips parting with the answer. What is it.

**BROKEN LEFT FOOT:** No one is stupid. Children aren't stupid, not even for for trying, like my son did, to jump off the top of the chain link climbing structure (12 feet high, at least). Kosta did it, sure, but he's small. "I landed on my foot and there was a crack." Sitting at St. Joseph's fracture ward, number in hand, waiting for attention. He will be diagnosed with a hairline fracture requiring a foot cast. But that's later: right now, our number is idling. I'm reading. I'm so hard reading and so angry that I don't have time to read, always interrupted by life. Angry I can't go faster. No way am I using my son's broken foot as an excuse for being unprepared. I need to finish this chapter in the next two hours. Focused so hard, I need to ignore him, bored out of his skull. I can't ignore a boy's boredom. "Take my phone," I said. He played stupid games and I read stupid history by a scholar whose name I now forget. Truth? I remember but it's too hard to explain. I remember buying him some chips and making him do some homework. And I helped him between readings.

**QUE SERA, SERA:** What is it? What is it? What was it, perhaps? What will it be? Will it be what it was or do we give up now? What will be, will be. Oh, Doris, shut up. What was it? What was it when it will be what it is? What will time do to it? What will I do to it, when time takes me? What is it here? What is the shape of this 'it'? The German *das ding*; the Freudian Thing; the stain in Lacan's hands. What is it, this stain? What stains you? What tain is that? Oh, the punctum of all that has happened. Camera. Da Da Camera. In camera. The silly polaroid. Stop it, Doris, said Betty.

**HISTORY AS METHOD:** If on a winter's night you had taken a different path. When? History is speechless but not wordless. The voice rims on the riff hours of speeches and silences. Hard soft. Tender tough. On off. Yes? "No," he said.

**PRE-MENOPAUSAL:** My sleepless nights. My blush and burn and sweat: was that just me sitting at Sweaty Betty's in the heat, thinking about who to approach for my committee? My mentors. Mentoring is so age-centric. What adults do to kids; what professors do for the nubile thoughts of an eager mind, forget the sexual persuasion. I am the eye that cuts her bangs alone, not a fruit worth 'tending.' Did I pass because they were sorry for me? Why hadn't I done this decades ago? They couldn't let me die while completing my degree so they moved me ahead? Am I being overly sensitive? Imagining things? Paranoid? Low self-esteem is the most inane diagnosis. This is not a noun, it is an excuse to fix it as quickly as one lifts the book: a bra that lifts it. Old and female, but not wise enough to estimate well. Having failed so much already, I shrank into my study cell.

**THE HOLE:** Trauma is a thing you wind around your mind so that you can't see it. It is a hole that is circled by the 'matter' of bone and flesh and muscle. In psychic terms, an illusion. But not unreal. In Freud's eyes, it was literally the *Das Ding* in the soup of the stomach of the unconscious. It passes through the mouth of the pre-conscious onto the floor of consciousness. The vomit is evidence of the 'event.' Badou's word for wound. Or there's another way to consider it, as Lacan does, when he introduces the 'real,' where the 'real' is an impossible thing (I've said this all before) that 'hits' the subject in the face. A basketball on the bridge of the glasses, between the eyes. I'm thinking Pound's "nor any pair showed anger / Saw eyes and stance between the eyes." A piece of the 'material' of this hit inspires Lacan's formula for trauma: the subject's relationship to what Lacan names "object a," becomes the 'fantasy' which, translated, is simply story. This is a story. The Pisan Cantos are history. Odysseus's long return was what? Dante's hell, which he knew very well. The 'event' of the thesis that won't come out, no matter how much I put down.

**EARLY CHRISTIAN HISTORY:** The Nail in some- one's coffin or the nail in Jesus's left foot: the function of the "nail" remains indeterminate. Provenance. Reliable witness. Because the function of this 'thing' to hang any hand or foot is without witness, history can rely on probability, only. On the spectrum of probabilities, history's fiction flows from all orifices. Her pastoral accents so different from our literary tongues, the shibboleths diachronically distinct... well, his- tory has no lesson for us. History is a subject, though, and we know that because she talks to us about the improbable provenance of Jesus' resurrection.

**FERAL CIRCLES:** A thousand nights I read and the cat sat, quietly curled on the chair above her food and water. She was just behind me. Her back was to the wall: she could study me. She studied me as I studied, reading from one book, and then the next. She and I shared this quiet space all through the winter, and even when my anxiety roared, it was focused inside under the light spilling over my hands, the pages of the book on the desk. I sat cross-legged; I sat in other sitting positions, yoga poses, sometimes stretching. I recall I did nothing else but sit and she watched my every move and dozed. At night I left the door open so she could roam the house. She circled every room on every floor while we slept. And in the day I was back at the desk and she was back in her chair. I didn't move and she didn't move though sometimes she got down to eat something, drink. I likely got up a lot, running to the bathroom, down to answer the door, to the kitchen to put dinner in the oven. Sure, I was a student, but mom first and foremost. And one day the tabby jumped down from her chair. I turned to her. She looked up at me. I turned back to my reading. Suddenly she was in my lap. One swift move and she had found the hole in my solitude.

**HER STORY:** Bury your head in the thousand deadheads. A stacked cemetery of roses gone to seed. He said, she said. Each one, a good hole for artichoke or salamander. Deep between the lips of never mind. The wind of fields folding winter into night. Schrodinger can see right through you, said Rasa, from her living room window. Is history speechless? Eternity rimmed that room with ears of silence; the way history rimmed the furnace; not at all the way the boy stopped on the road looking at the girl walking home. Very deep down between the streets.

**HIS STORY:** His story is that he wants to be a lumberjack but his dad is CEO of a conglomerate. Yes, he couldn't get further north than this "small-town" university because of his dad. Maybe he was lying to me. History is fiction, after all. Not. It is not. Why not? It is not fiction because it is method. What is history then? It takes what is there, it digs and routes around. It steps back and thinks; where does this fall under the spectrum of actual to probable to "I don't know." What happened? I don't know. I sat on the couch where he wanted me to lie down. I could not lie. I could not say what happened. I sat and said that. I asked him: "will I ever know?" "Impossible to say," said the analyst.

**MODES OF MEMORY:** Citations are ethics in the factory of knowing. Good memory bad. Discourse and discuss. But did you not realize that academia is another version of capitalism: with every book you publish, you are never rich enough? You cannot be too thin or rich enough; you cannot be too published or thin enough. Something was disgusted, I have the footnote to prove discourse. Method please. Which way? This way please. Don't touch. No photographs, can't you read? On the rim of voices and the vault, that deep chasm of institutional time, catching with all her openings, mouth and ears and even eyes. Can you hear it, how well history remembers? A tool for learning. Discipline as method. So maybe history teaches us nothing because it is just a way of walking. At least it remembers the function of an "I" of subjectivity as it goes. Descartes's cogito. Read closely here.

**WHAT IS WILD:** My history is wild. She is my love who plays with birds and gifts them to me, "no thanks, we don't want your salamander here." My disapproval makes love lope away, head down. The signifying struggle of the gift, Derrida said. Forget speech, how much ash do you trace in the archive of days you didn't count? My monster breath and the left hand, not even a hole, but a basket for her beautiful eyes.

**WINTER AGAIN:** There was a wonderful night in the dark when the man dressed himself in snowfall as he left history at home to walk to the corner store. It's interesting that voices thrown from dead dimensions have life and men walk away from history as method. This indicates nothing specific. Except distance, or is it space? Better than the speed of pedestrian thought. Rimming as in "Drive." Does history drive? Does history have a car? Can history walk to the corner store because we need milk for the coffee? A voice thrown across the night, folding in the book and left for dead. Deep deep down between the sheets, between and inside the fold of lips. If history drives, my wild is a dog.

**THESIS:** Windows everywhere so you can look in. What did he say? What's the question? He answered, "No" and a hole opened beneath my feet. "What do you think [you're doing here]?" My Katabasis.

# RIMS OF THE DEFENCE

**DISCIPLINE 4:** In my department, I chose my fields of study. What fields are you working in; what grows on your field and is it worth eating? Better yet, what's the perspective; do you look through the trees around a bowl, or do you lord it over the townsfolk from towers of appropriated ivory? Or are you QC, admonishing the conquest of foreign gold? Fields lying fallow, fields of hybrid research, fields of trauma, fields of secularism, fields of postcolonial suffering. Decolonize this. To think one geographical formation can be used for any research; equal to how discipline becomes a discipline, and through discipline the institution houses professionals who engage in 'discourse' about (as opposed to discuss) that discipline. Field here describes the geography of the language; discourse a landscape of the mind; colonizing and landmines; the texture of explosions is brilliant, any poet will tell you. I am thinking of Dionne Brand's *Theory*. I am also thinking of the words one scholar used about my work: ambitious. Ambitious is, perhaps, a non-sexist, non-ageist adjective. Only for those who are deniers. Is it good? No. Ambitious means I can see your underwear (fail); in other words, good try, but no cigar; in short, your explosive fizzled. I like to think 'ambitious' has no gender, sex or ageist privileges. But how would I know. I am not a good example. I had a PhD defence with all the proper people and we had two rounds of interrogation, yes, one less than might be considered standard, and that was followed by the 'in camera.' Where they go to decide my fate. When we convened, the show was done.

**SALVAGE:** How good it feels, this salvaged edge. No there to the edge. No here to the wedge, that part between the round-table and the square of my defence. They took their seats while I sat, disarmed, the bull for slaughter. You don't know how good it feels to run my finger along the edge of this burnt flank, feel the ash crumble from this hole. To shed the rot. My first house and my last hole, in terms of timing, burning still in terms of rubber, so durable and resistant to pain. I love red. In retrospect, so polyester.

**START AT THE TOWER AND TURN LEFT:** A defence should be rimmed by high fences and happy delegates cheering. The only charring is a woman who was paid less than minimum wage. A channel brimming with drinks and a barbecue, why not. Hibbatchi anyone? On the defence line, it's Saturday and we are dreaming that the camera caught us naked. Shit. How can you defend your body parts when you have been objectified by people at the campfire? The camera is on fire. The stake is charbroiled. Let's try another corn cob and wait for December. The red red gaze rimming the table, Pamplona is there to make that animal so tired he can only gore the matador. Don't get me started. Fade to blood.

**SETTLE THE BILL:** My katabasis. A bull descending to her destiny. Fuck it, just wear white. My wide arms are unwavering in their call to Tiresias who will answer and admit nothing. Where did Ulysses go? Fend off the terror, I cannot see where I'm going. A hole in the forest, mid-way, a mid-day, where children should not go. Dante's circle of hell, this must be a joke. So, I settle and listen to the questions, the deflections, the cryptic traps, the weird, weird silence. Where can I run and why is there no red red here? Do you see what I mean? There was nothing to see, because they changed the game. Easing into the finish.

*VENI VIDI VICI*: Circling of what has 'passed,' smoke rings outline what used to be human on the floor. Body of events. Red lips smile. Bodices and Botticelli. If only. The rim of life on the trim of a window coffining a time and place, circling on a saw-ed up world, while fingers try to work a tacky light-switch. Stick. Stick. Why won't this open? I don't know how to say it, but everything is yellow now. Jaundice. Sulfuric.

**SHALLOW DAUGHTERS:** The camera is crammed with bullshit. The camera is a fine fisherman, a chase and leap at the Roadrunner, but that comes after the fourth season, stitching the lake of our discussion, all the reasons to define a pass. To get from A to B. No. A to A+. And afterwards, we will see what the camera caught: the animal all whaled like Jacob in the bible, swallowed whole. Oh my disaster, dis of the stars tonight. The camera hooks the children with its simulations. And we have heard there was running through the streets. Easy does it. The bull is testy.

**SELAH:** Apparently, there are too many bouncing *Das Dings*. Ah. *a.* Maybe that's my desire for the A + I clawed at, again and again. The still life of a bowl I wanted to feed on, to the brim with apples, vegetables, a bull in the museum. What balls to eat pure concept. Too many roads and tape marks lacing the boots that tread where angels fear. These roads went winding round the lack, tape marks across the floor of the blue DSM. So I moreovered. Or moored. To discuss the holes I dug, wherever I could, I furthermored. Mirrored with a thoughtful knife.

## THE STORES ARE SHUTTERED FOR SIESTA:

Circle twice and convene the camera, as in a bullfight. I was unprepared or I had no red light, nor *arret-toi*. There was no running, no jabbing or joisting, no smiling either. Sticks, sure, but small and nothing went deep enough. No one held it up; everyone held it close and shut up. The shutter of the balls of this game of defence, or little blades, rimmed and rhyming so tightly. A kind of Dr. Seuss, it made me laugh, so that suddenly, it was done. Time to convene for the photo shoot. Not photogenic I thought someone would give me the other cheek, the right side, or have my back. It was "I," Terisias, the bull who saw everything but was missing the point. The Matador had double-booked and needed to get downtown fast. There was no proud death.

**CAN YOU HEAR ME NOW?** When tires start burning they don't stop—a veritable endless source of combustion and endless venting of venom, traversing the fantasy of mobility, infiltrating stratospheres and centuries, from Damascus, Milan, Salamanca and Calabria, all the human rubbish, reaching the ozone and knocking madly. Vision of a chick knocking at the ceiling of her home for her newborn freedom. The disease of global indigestion at this table where disaster plays, a red Sharpie and paper. When we all stood up and moved from the arena where the ball rolled, the dropping of it, the bouncing and the ping pong of some very very very 'real' (Oh, said Lacan) ratatatat burning *Ding*. Do you know what I mean by that smell of disavowal? Selah.

**I WISH YOU WERE HERE:** *Wo Es war, soll Ich werden.* Take this shrimp and bite into its parsley bikini, unconcerned by the nakedness of bitter herbs that will seep into the crevices of reversals and perversions of straight balls and tight little 'a's, artichokes or antecedents, bullfights and auto-dafes. My teeth hurt. I wore white as a defence but in retrospect I realize, I was a swab. Pausing here to smell the pot-lights. A crime, someone argues, and others say don't be so melodramatic. To dress for a date, having signed the bill of sale in advance, with no Helen, or Paris, no Tiresias or Penelope, no Florence where Beatrice was born. To read no wine, smell no kiss, and taste the indefensible. Betty, I am Tiresias: they took my eyes out and just left.

**IN CAMERA:** When the 'in camera' of the defence was finished, assuming that nothing of what had been said remained, though I saw ash everywhere in the room when I returned to my "pass," one of my advisors turned to me, with her hand full of my hair, and said: "what do I do with this now?" I did not at the time recall, but I see it now: that day when I was 12, in Florence, sitting in the piazza, very tired of walking, and turning to see Perseus in the distance, holding Medusa's head in his hands, a sword at his side. I felt so deeply that was something for me: I would be Perseus. I didn't know about Cixous, yet. A woman laughing at the man who couldn't get it up for a woman who, purportedly, killed her children. A woman full bodied and prolific, unlike any man. Cixous embracing her gendered body. So here is that Perseus at my defence, holding my screaming snakes in her hand. A woman with a sword who couldn't stand not understanding me. A kind of disgust with my mind. In her philosopher hands my head, subway cars chaptering the argument, virtually resting there, a treasure of the lost that I had found. This was a PhD, gifted to everyone. Brick that I am, I bluffed, "It's your copy." That is, do with it as you want. Medusa-me — I didn't see her pitch my snakes, 500 pages of it, into the recycling. How could I? She threw my head to the floor. I laughed and stepped on it. I bluffed and walked right into it. My defence was an empty net. Those strands of thought could have been used to bring down this place. One part of me was squired again; one part of me roared into the station.

# THE STAR OF REDEMPTION

"Starting with a hole"
– Lacan, "The Subversion of the Subject"

**HAVING PASSED:** I sat with an empty box on my knees on the subway, numb. I arrived home to a dark house, everyone asleep, and put the box down. Touching the floor a knife into my world, the hole of my life without her. So shot down by grief I didn't hear my thesis slip out and circle the house, circle my heart, and settle for her eternal rest.

**COGNITIVE DISSONANCE:** "No," he said. Why not? I don't understand what you're trying to do. No, said Rosenzweig at the eleventh hour, when he realized he could not convert to Christianity: in his heart, he was a Jew. No, that's not what I mean. Why not?

**VANITY:** Looking into the mirror for age spots, discolouration, sagging jowls, long before losing eyebrow hairs (who knew that would ever be an issue?!), remembering the professor friend of the family who asked me: "well, will it be okay for you to get your degree at the age of 50?" I sat there on my ass, thinking of that number, saying "Sure, I don't see why not!" Not understanding that time is a mathematical formula sold by Clinique and other brands to replenish collagen, erase age spots. That time is different for men. Not doing the math on the fact that misogyny is hale and wealthy still.

**LAW OF MORTALITY:** There's a kind of shortening of the gene that leads to the failure of life to regenerate: the law of aging. An old woman is a monster in the academy. A foreshortening of her foot in the academic door. I look, shocked to see a crease above my lip suddenly appear. This is only the beginning of bleeding lipstick. I will enter my defence at the sea swell of my end.

## UNSPOKEN LAW OF ACADEMIC FERTILITY:

I didn't understand that my role as teacher was not as a model of thought, but a Vogue centerfold. The students look at what I wear; they locate every crease in my cotton, in my flesh. I am plaster, crumbling under the sheer power of their stare. They listen then shame me if I don't know what Tinder is. I am so not woke. I hear about a younger female professor getting a nip and tuck on her features, so as to outsmart the law of the academic jungle. I do what I can to nip and tuck myself into their culture. Not doing the math on how I am a woman without tenure, long past the period of academic fertility. Earlier, I could not do the math on the unspoken law of ageism in misogyny. Or am I blaming everyone else for the simple fact that I have been proceeding despite disabilities for years. It takes longer to do anything when you're faking able.

**PASSING:** I am alone in a big room at the Animal hospital, waiting to hear from the doctor about Phil Phil, my almost-a-dog once feral tabby. I can't get through to my husband. There's no service back here, between Yonge Street and McMurrich. I'm sitting in a chair by a window, all the space of me reflected in the dark glass. This is a huge room for just one person. I roam around it, sit in different chairs, consider the extended families that could be accommodated here, eight sitting, more standing, all consulting the doctor about the dog's kidney, the cat's eyes. "Phil Phil," says the vet, "has saddle thrombus." "What's that?" "A stroke in the artery where the hind legs join. Surgery…" I stopped listening then. My mind's eye watching her front paw scramble up the stairs to hide: a wild animal, finding a quiet, dark place, to die.

**LAWS OF LIFE:** Dr. Nasser insisted nothing is created or destroyed so Phil Phil's spirit remains with us, after her death. The bones animating my pepper radiance demands the question: where did she go? Monster, I was her mom, when she was in the mood, brushing my face against her head... my history is a shambles. Devastated by this rent in life of inimitable... Her purr, caged by her ribs, from deep to so very deep.

**MY DISASTER:** Circling her last breath, she holes my fabric, a rip a tear a cry of katabasis. She passed out. The pass. Passing the fantasy. History should be read as the history of my love for her. Stop! A scream echoes because nothing is created or destroyed. She passed out before she passed. She passed out on the carpet. The pattern is empirically sound, even if it is a little deterministic. Very so, deep down deep inside. Beginning with holes, between everything.

MY LOVE: In my dream I am all good except the end of my torso, where my legs should be. I see the frayed ends of some electric wire. History is this long story of faulty wiring, if we are, as the psychotic, Daniel Paul Schreber attested, simply energy circuits. If we are energy, regulating light in our dreams. If we are a summer of material, she was a basket through which love shines. Conditionals abound. An inner rim, a hidden thimble of pain that roared up the spine.

**ANOTHER ORBIT:** circled the room and then collapsed on the carpet, uneasily. So much love has traced these rooms; so many faces in the spines and talking heads around me. The clacking of rheumatism remembered by the wood she traced, around the rooms, up and down the stairs. Hearing things. Jesus and Paul are in her, an immortality that piled itself into my arms, my lap, my life, my hold and settled into her empty box banging on my thighs from the hospital, down the street to the subway, on my lap to home. It is dark, but for a single light left on for me. I put the box down and Derrida, Kaufman, Copernicus and Lacan fall to their knees and wail.

# LAWS — OR *NOMOS CHRISTOS*

"But even without the Law, I was once alive. But when the commandment appeared, the Thing flared up, returned once again, I met my death. And for me, the commandment that was supposed to lead to life turned out to lead to death, for the Thing found a way and thanks to the commandment seduced me; through it I came to desire death."

— Lacan, *Seminar VII*

**CONFERENCE:** I attended a conference as an outsider. I attended a conference knowing the audience was very much like a scholar who refused to work with me. So I came to biblical studies scholarship my own way, using Lacan mixed with Derrida/Spivak and Badiou/Zizek not to mention Benjamin. And I came with the handicap of not having a mentor who could escort me in; of mixing disciplines and weakening them. When I got to the conference, there was one woman, a beautiful sweet nun, who I had met years before working on the television documentary series on biblical studies. She recognized me immediately. For a moment there was light.

## CONFERENCES ARE ALWAYS AWKWARD:

The nun recognized me and sat down beside me, asking how I'd been. I felt so embraced. Perhaps she had read my application for the Department's Tenure Track position in Early Christianity. I was all Paul, after all. As the day progressed, the first day, which was the day for my presentation, I realized everyone in the room, every presenter except for that renegade graduate student doing critical theory at Guelph and the precocious graduate student in the department who was obviously being mentored by three of the six professors in the audience, all of us untenured scholars had skin in the game. We were being screened: this conference was the forum for the profs to shape a 'short list' of applications for the 'real' interview.

**THE JOB MARKET:** There were jobs and there were no jobs. There were jobs, he said. There will be jobs, she said. There were no jobs before and I worked in the mines all those years and even I found a job. There will be jobs. The sun cuts the rim of her tooth. Blood breaks. There will be jobs. Suck it up. "I'll drive," she said. "Stop," we cried. The deer missed us and the tire rim flew into the sun. "I notice, there are no jobs," Kierkegaard said. "There is no repetition," Deleuze replied. Everything is repetition.

**WHAT DID PAUL SAY?:** "There is no difference between a Jew and a Gentile." I should have started with that. It would have explained what I mean when I say that *Nomos Christos*, The Law of Christ, replaces death. That is the law of mortality. I could have added, yes, I look old, but all the better to grasp Paul's law.

**WHAT IS IT, THIS NOMOS CHRISTOS?:** I arrive at the conference podium armed with many laws. They keep sliding from my hands, or no, I'm shuffling a deck of cards and the ace of spades keeps flying into the audience. I am digging my own grave. Betty, who is me, recounts: "they say that Paul says blah blah blah." She pauses. I pause. "That is the law blah blah," she continues. "No, I mean the law blah blah blah." Meanwhile gravity pulls another apple from her breast. Or the law of wind. Of death. "No, the Law blah blah," she repeats. They are not following. "Let me explain difference: there is the deferral in a semantic sense, and there is difference." What is she getting at? "Let me explain." Betty is at the podium, her skirt hiked up, her underwear all over her face. The pin that kept up her hem slipped out, dropped to the floor. Everyone heard the unravelling.... She turns red and steps down. No one offers a hand. I am watching as a pigeon under a hungry hawk whose talons, nicely tucked as per the etiquette of animal kingdom, bleeds me of life. This stem of genius breaks off.

**BREAKING THE LAW:** Betty breaks winter and changes the order of things, a self-identified Kepler with a finger on the constellations. She breaks the law of academic debt, causing a scholar to throw her head to the desk—a—a—ashamed for Betty declaiming imbecilic outdated scholarship with her skirt hiked over her underpants. Things in the wrong order. Coffee ground into the carpet. I'm betting that the coffee break was necessary after *Nomos Christos* was carted out, though there was nothing illegal about what she did and the petite fours. Cubic laws and desire. O do not fall for gravity. Do not stop for Death, though Paul of Tarsus did, and then came back, a new man. We should be so lucky, resurrected in this marvellous scholarship. Bitter k-ni-gh-t.

*NACHTRAGLICHKEIT:* German for 'afterwardsness.' Or another word for return. It is so right to give consonantal shape to the psychic wound, its edges jagged, rough and cutting, unforgotten. Careful is the approach—you might step on it and destroy its provenance. So much tongue and lip to the ache. "No," he said. What did he say? No, that's not what I meant. Yet things were said. ""I said nothing, she said. "No," someone added, "that's not what I meant." And the scholar threw her face into her hands, ashamed for Betty. Stupid Betty. K-nigh-t... K-nigh-t.... This jagged, rough, cutting edge feels so right.

**ALL TRAUMA:** The room circled me and I circled back. Not the way a circus comes to town, but the lady who came and never sang. No, there was a massive tree in the room, and I am destined to be that K-nigh-t, Tancred, killing Clorinda for the second time. *Nachtraglichkeit.*

**STATE VIOLENCE:** Walter Benjamin meditates on violence and the state. It is the only means of enforcing laws; in the case of good laws the violence to maintain those laws is good, though controversial. Then Spivak picks that up off the floor, and using chewing gum, attaches it to scholarship, which she claims is violent: it violates by cutting. The law of a discipline being to keep your limbs inside the lines. I can feel the million cuts, to eternity, in my transgressing disciplinary borders. Each slash a Tancred on my bark. Oh, I keep forgetting: I'm Tancred, and the speaking wound of the tree is the mirror of my self-cutting. What discipline is this? It took me so long to get here, wherever here is.

**DARWIN IN THE ACADEMIC JUNGLE:** I arrive at the podium of this conference, armed with many laws. Faking it till I drop. The imperialist mask keeps sliding from face, my hands keep poking Agamemnon's eyes to keep my thoughts straight. I am at the podium, my skirt hiked up, my underwear all over my face, a spade in my hand, a trough below. You can hear a pin drop... I turn red and step down. No one offers a hand. I am a pigeon under a hungry hawk whose talons, nicely tucked as per the etiquette of the animal kingdom, bleed me of life. At least there is something natural about this.

**LAWLESS WEST:** In Canada, there is a law that allows you to go topless. There are so many laws to keep order, such as those that keep us from colliding on the streets. There is the unspoken law of academic success and the law of the capitalist jungle. There are laws against abuse, but there is no law to keep the wolves from the door. The law about not letting your dog piss on the grass—likely just a bylaw, if at all. The bylaw not to play music loud past 11 pm. One law for us settlers and and one law for all the first nations.

**CLOSE READING OF TIME:** In that café named Mercurio, I predicted that the future of trauma in Canada would be centered on Indigenous culture. At the time, my thinking seemed to come out of nowhere but in retrospect I see that I was simply drawing a line from a *Globe and Mail* story about Regina back in 2005 to 2012 and watched it extend into the future. The article shared photos of rooms with no heating; windows with no glass; floors with no carpet; sinks with no running water; empty closets except for used syringes. In 2012, I could see nothing had changed. The critique of trauma by post-colonialism that would eventually become decolonization ripped through intellectual practice in humanities and would tear disciplines to shreds. English was the heaviest casualty. But back then, in 2012, when English was still strong, my supervisor looked at me over his coffee as if to say: would you consider exploring trauma in Indigenous literature? I hadn't started my dissertation. There was time to shift from the biblical period to the present. As if I could smell the push against white superemacy coming, I said: "I wouldn't pursue scholarship on the trauma of Indigenous culture. I could, sure. But that's not right, to take work that's not mine." I felt like Blanchot, taking a position in front of the firing squad. I was doing the right thing, but had the privilege of my apparent whiteness to be saved regardless.

**SCHOLARLY VIOLENCE:** I am pretty good at spinning the laundry in with the dishes and throwing nothing out. Foolish words that might have got caught in the gears. Sound of a laugh, perhaps. I died in Christ, Paul said. If only I had died there, on the spot, I wouldn't have had to lug my Golden Ass off the stage. Stupid Betty, fell into the grave she had dug. She noticed the bones of all these ancient laws, ruins of artless intelligence. Man to ass to Betty falling down. Picasso's Women of Avignon, with no faces to speak. The violence of each experiment. Dante's hell is an upside down cake. It didn't take her long to complete a revolution of her katabasis.

**BETTY SAID:** I am strong when I am weak. Yes, we're still at the conference. Hard to haul yourself out of the hole you fell into. You can hang a heavy argument on things. The law of Christ is Paul's fiction: a hole for a man-made button. Try pulling yourself up on that. "Obviously, this hurts me more than you," she said, retreating to the coffee table. "I dream of your heaven," said the spoon. Yes. It's my fault she fell from the light, without a word, pushing down her skirt. Everything was dark again.

**SESSIONAL PROFESSOR:** A mature woman with a doctorate, holding a job for a limited term... with no future. She doesn't know it yet, as if Phil Phil's departure initiates some kind of hard ending in the academy. This is not a memoir of my life as a cat owner: my life as a mother; my life as a woman; my life as someone who calls her mood disorder failure. This is a memoir of a person who accomplished something, while living a life, loving her son, her cat, and her research, in an institution that appeared to be dying. Something is wrong with this thing she has done. Or maybe what was wrong was hiding the way she feels and thinks, which would have explained why she arrived, long after her generation set sail.

**SHAME:** "My Agamemnon mask was fake," Betty said. Underwear all over her face. The shame roared. It roared of ad hominem, or Niagara Falls. The plant that processed salt so fresh dinner was inedible. Shellac on the job market. It roared with categorical anguish, lionizing the point, red meat of the question: who did Paul really meet on the road to Damascus? Is that your thesis question? Betty's projectile vomit all over the audience. Not really, but close enough.

PERSPECTIVE: The wound of this imperialist beast of humanities smells: now on its side, breathing rapidly, the elephant in the room is ready for the mercy shot before being buried quickly to avoid contamination. Everyone ignores her, which lets her pain prolong. Who wants to be called a murderer of a massive tradition? Absolving themselves of violence by disavowing what lies at their feet, they beat it to their corner of the universe, stricking their heads in the sand of an imperative to publish. I am right there, beside them, busy with my failures, smelling something. If I can smell it so profoundly, why can't they? Maybe they have gotten used to the rot.

## THE FUTURE PERFECT IS NOT AT FAULT:

Listening to Hamlet declaring, "Something is rotten in the state of Denmark" I envision the tragedy of institutional twighlight. The future is inevitable (tautologies abound). Why will English Departments in US colleges shut down? Rot is inevitable. Let me interject with my foot in the door of history. Will the door hold or is that rotting, too? Why is that student who would be a brilliant English scholar enrolled in business administration? Not an anomaly but the pattern of a fundamental rot. For example, in the winter of 2021, Laurentian University will have closed down 69 undergrad and graduate programs, the majority of those being in the humanities. 116 tenured faculty at Laurentian will have lost their jobs. The closures will not have been about just money, will they? It is the impossible: the law of tenure is dying. For those who will have lost their jobs, it will not have been about just money. It will have been about the mortality of an institution. For those who are precariously employed, now and in the future, it is the law of survival. Nothing's perfect. Why aren't we already over at the Schulich School of Business, meeting Musk, greeting Gates, chewing on the bone of a good steak in the next business plan? Meanwhile, back to the future, the English beast will have rolled over and just refused to get up. What discipline could if it will have found itself stuck in the gutter of composition courses? Depressing, isn't it? Thus English, as a fruit on the humanities tree, will have rotted from the inside out. A Hamlet moment pondering the ghost of imperialism. Not even interdisciplinarity will resurrect you.

# WHAT HAPPENED?

**NO, HE SAID:** The hole you carry everywhere you go, Linus. He said no and did not say what he meant. Many exchanges of holes in the meantime. The question of fail. Epic fail. Pass me in the halls and jump high. Pass me the salt, I am sick in the heart. I passed. I passed through the gates and they shut behind me. 99, help me out. I am not Smart, but I get it. This too will pass and other depressions. I am hubris, folded into letters no one will open. The Ph., the D. bonding all Agamben's witnesses to Badiou's event. The conferring of Cunegonde in the Lisbon streets. The archive relies on eternity: there will always be time to find what has been discarded. Eternity of the cat's life, or 9 of them, one in me. Deep deep down between openings and departures, letters, numbers. Everyone, plus one. *Anche, mille e tre.* Anus, ears and mouth through which I catch birds passing. Lacan moved his topology from words to letters to numbers, hooks and eyes of the Borromean knot, settling into the 'sinthome'. Eat it, the rim of your shambles. Ha, deep so very deep beneath the folds of my ache, I hear your birds singing tiny holes in the night. My sweet, dream me all over again.

**N.V.:** Discipline is a kind of "feeling it before you know it" thing. It is the house into which you walk, smelling the olive oiled linoleum, the nicotine walls, baked apple pork in the carpet and yesterday's beef bourguignon between the sofa seams. All of this living marinating in sweat and tears. Is there a dog here, somewhere? You can feel the light in this place, and know, with all these living smells, this is where you want to be; not to eat, but to size it up and down, because you know this room is good. Maybe Goldilocks, looking for her 'mean.' It doesn't matter. What matters is that when you arrive, you are mentally nubile, with very few juvenile notions of what you're feeling; you know how not to be caught in the imaginary. So when you start, they will either not take you seriously (because you aren't hormonally lush enough to warp) or will ignore you because you are thick with methodological fallacies such as 'feeling' and 'instinct,' the skills of someone who has been around the block, forget the disorders. Advisors suggesting not to mention your creative work. Others advising in very oblique terms, not to admit your unfitness for the job, i.e. those disorders, mood, eating, other. One flank will pass you in the halls not seeing you, since you stand as no direct threat to the little corner of that field that is their domain. This indifference, even as you excel in courses, take authority when you talk (not all the time), and always forget to avoid the categorical (ha!). When you come out the other side, you will not be young enough so will be labeled too 'ambitious' to be a professional. Who knew that age was the follow up to chronic failure; that the shame of youth could return, with wrinkles; that a woman of a certain age faces the universal border sooner and with more on her shoulders. That's discipline for you, a closed world that admits only those who can be tempered by their youth because age is for reclining in villas beside full pastures, being fed (yes, passive) the delectables of their labour, falling from the vines where the young can do the all-nighters collecting, collating, archiving. Juvenile scholars, an army of harvesters accumulating in the institutions, jam-packed.

**NOTHING:** Paul was a disciple. He never met the living Jesus. He was older than the other 'true' disciples, true because they knew Jesus when he was alive: Matthew, Mark, John, oh and etc. Paul was a real follower because he encountered the truth of Christ, personally, as the resurrection. Paul applied discipline to himself when spreading the 'good news' of the Doxa, the light that breaks the greatest most trenchant border, the one between life and death. Paul was a disciplinarian of eternal life, who argued that circumcision, another discourse border, another shibboleth in the bath-house, could be executed in your heart. How do you navigate the small organ, the tower of stairs and windows, life smells of disappointment, desire, failure, lack, all while it demands things? So many steps to perform "discipline" that when I complete the walk of shame, again and again, I face the truth that I have accomplished the professionalization of an anachronism. The worlding of this ground by the raging earthquake of critical race theory, disabilities studies, Indigenous studies, burying the colonizer's English literature, breathtaking to watch. How do you tell them that academia is not crumbling, it is a force being liberated from all jurisdictions of privilege that have been held in place by the beast of tradition. To think I am a whole harvest of discourse that is irrelevant to this new place, audible only for my eternal Phil Phil. Ex nihilo, I am standing in a field of rot, ergo, nothing.

**I DID NOT WAKE UP, ONE DAY, TOO OLD FOR THIS:** I am not a dinosaur. Tyrannosaurus. I did not spend years having fun playing monsters with light and fingers. I am this old because I couldn't keep my borders straight; others, my own; tried to suck it up, but kept falling back down the hill, misunderstanding or just not strong enough? Saw a lot in climbing again and again, decade after decade; am old according to the misogynist industries, can smell rot years before it will have come, but inside, I'm still ten, wondering why bad things happen.

**NOTHING HAPPENED.** No thing. *Das ding.* That's the thing, no?

# NACHTRAGLICHKEIT #1 — FAST

*"Much food stored in a cool cave"*

**THESIS:** I crammed my mouth with discipline, jamming the pores, the hair, nose and eyes. Full to the brim. I accept the fault.

**THESIS:** She broke the rules and laughed at Adam's rib. Bone of a corset of colonization. Nothing natural about breaking bread. Sometimes state violence is necessary. Bread crumbs. Pass the salt, please. There's a lake of ice in your head. Not all the cold of a winter day goes around the lake. I can't tell you how sharp the sky, cutting light so the eyes rim and I can see all the way around my face. "Drive," she said. "Stop," we cried. Katabasis as a cliff. Deep into the belly of Tiresias. Blind is Katabasis. Darkness deep into the belly of. Belly's up. Jellyfish and katabasis. Katabasis is dark, blinding Tiresias.

**THESIS:** They all talked. The room talked. The talking was a sound around the room. No talking please. They talked anyway. She talked. They all talked, talked, talked. No Talking Please. Ok, let's whisper. They talked in a whisper. They whispered about Paris. Schleimann couldn't take it anymore. They talked about that. Remembered to whisper, "I told you so." Stop it, you're driving me crazy. They talked about uptight people and gathered their books. They left talking. Then in the silence, the thunder said: *I am I and Betty is she, and Betty is me, sometimes.*

**THESIS:** Betty's dress is wide. Betty's Freud smiles. Contempt, a continent of discontent, a dark continent. The darkness of Betty's insides. Lacan is late, again. Betty's driving. The turn is sharp. The shark mind of Freudean slips. The soft slide of wide tides. The dig. Watch your step. The wide smile of Betty's skirt. The grid of Lacan's act. It's sharp. No, it's soft. No. It's a step. Watch your step. It's a turn. Mind your foot. Johannes was here. It's the car in which Betty drives that is wide as a continent. She'll never make it. The distance between one ocean and another. Mind the gap, she heard. Cut.

**THESIS:** Masada housed a baker and many pigeons. The baker's stone oven and ash. Pigeon holes. The holy ash of a baker's dozen. The flight and return. The ash of his letter. Return to sender as undeliverable. Don't pigeon that stone. The ash of shit on the stone. The bullshit of a baker's oven. The dozen or so holes for each pigeon. The shit here is ancient. The bones? Sticks, not bones, I think. The hole in the sky through which pigeons go and return. The message is not whole. The fragment of stone thought. The fragments. The splitting. The splitting of the time between baking and reading. When does she have time to write?

**THESIS:** It took Paul three years to 'come out' with his revelation that that light was (had to have been/ will have been?) Jesus: who did Paul really meet on the road to Damascus? Is that your thesis question? Betty's projectile vomit all over the Roman toilet.

**THESIS:** Plough and grade. Plough and sleep. Plough the fields again, they're a mess. Plough the bread. Plough the grades. Plough through sleep. *Again. They looked everywhere for the truth of Jesus in the Dead Sea Scrolls.* Grade and plough. Sleep and plough. The mess of fields to plough, or was that sweep? The bread of plough and then break for ploughman's lunch. The grades of a pint. The sleep of the pub. The plough and no man.

**THESIS:** I'll tell you, I smelled ash in the air of my "pass." The external position turned as everyone here turns as if always at a turning point, or want to be, with one hand full of Agamemnon's mask. I am not Schliemann, I wanted to say, as a joke, you know, to add some oxygen. Was interrupted: "what do I do with this now?" These strands of lake and summer never worn.

**THESIS:** A as the article; a as the object; A as the aleph; ach, I don't understand. Anterior thoughts or the future anterior of the moon in Scorpio; antipathy and postmodern sociopath; auntie, why are you late again? We have missed you. Anthills and anemones; art and ass; assuage the apple of my eye; aster, artichoke, and amplify, ambling down the asphalt. Betty, go catch her before she salads everything. Ach, I'm choking.

**THESIS:** Benjamin had 17 pieces to his thesis. I have lost count of mine. The one thesis into which every part falls and is the haunting of that Montreal night when too many ghosts wandered in and wouldn't stop talking. What is it? Your thesis, I mean. What is it?

**THESIS:** So much sand too much *objet* cause of desire, was the critique. Words with salt. As if this were a meal and the complaint was that the salt had fallen off the shelf into the mix. The wound of her thinking, all over the place. Too many lost causes. Shimmer in the bowl of Eden's forbidden tenderloin, aleph of my heart, artichokes and clover. I did them myself, Betty confessed; they tasted alright. All by myself. The day they noticed the good neighbour wasn't there.

**THESIS:** My stars my stars, I tell you nothing compares to the *jouissance* of tears scrimming—no, I meant screaming in your face. Red as sunset, scarlet of Pacino's face, the alpha scar purloined by the fascist jerk. Hormones running free along the hills of Derrida's Marxist ghosts, stolen and spoken for, messianic. Thus spoke Zarathustra through the halls of this institution. And pigeons should be so lucky, washing with dirt.

**THESIS:** Hemingway, because America or Paris. And Stein, we love you. My bird played crazy eights around the pastry shelves. Remember Betty, beating eggs into the fast lane around that hairline curve where the ice…? Blanchot and with him, Kofman. Let me cut you a quarter for your thoughts, lemon and sugar. Spivak Derrida. Look up into the window and see that blue light when eight falls over and goes eternal. You probably think this is about you, Kierkegaard. Let me outline the many threads to each reading of Kierkegaard on repetition. There was chocolate. Repeating myself, Lacan. The psychoanalyst said nothing but cut deeply.

**THESIS:** To laugh the way the wine. There was no wine. To sling the way the grape, around and around. There was never a vine. To monster debt, immaculate and bitch. To arrive at my defence and find Blanchot's eternity had etched the walls with testimony, or did I fall for the lights? The soldiers got up and left. Did they come prepared with bullets? Waiting, defenceless. Come back Zarathustra, I need you to measure again. Measure once and blame yourself for accidents twice. Second time the farce of existential angst. Face it. What? There was no wine and on the surface, no grounds for coffee. The ice went round and round. Deep deep deep down inside the tablecloth of another century.

**THESIS:** I would not stop, said Emily, wearing tulle. The drive to hell and back. Dante, we missed you and narrative-wise, dawn breaks. Birthdays return and we remember. "I'm five" he announces, so proud. "Never to do that again." Blanchot's single encounter with eternity. Conversion is such a misnomer for change: Paul returns with good news; Paul turns to ask me why I'm bothering. Better to use Metanoia, the Greek for change, from this frail human frame to the immortal, of dying and living in Christ. Ovid's *Metamorphosis*, you see. Deep deep deep down between these lids and lips, rising. Swim, Copernicus, swim faster. Kepler is coming.

**THESIS:** The dissing of the lights, the spinning of the table, the aim of each interrogative always slightly off, the silences cracking the day open in wide canyons of eternal time. Rosenzweig starts with death, just like Paul. "Stop," she said. Marx, where are you? "I have been waiting forever for this to stop," she said. Derrida's interest in lacunae reached the corners of their effort. And where the wheel of splendour stopped, camer-errata knows. Listening so hard to what she would not recognize. Would it come as a kind of thunder, drum roll, the launch of NASA aircrafts into space, the sharp precision of God's chosen-ness? Betty had never been here before, had no idea what she was to listen for. Falling in. If what happened was anything like anything she could have imagined, then it was nothing. I am a grain of sand, light-headed and waiting for the sky to fall. What is the sound of a star falling? Will you answer? Will you?

**THESIS:** He declines Greek, which renders History speech-less. This would suggest history speaks.

**THESIS:** Nail in the coffin or the nail in Jesus's left foot: the function of this "nail" remains indeterminate. Provenance. Reliable witnesses. Because the function of this 'thing' to hang any hand or foot is without witnesses, history can rely on probability, only. On the spectrum of probabilities, history's fiction flows from all orifices.

**THESIS:** Oh Clorinda—a voice of the dead, killed again. She is a tree in a forest accusing her fiancé of murder. This is the fiction from Tancred's head. The story symbolic of Tasso's, the 'author' 's, trauma. Does history remember being killed or killing? If so, where is her memory located? In the tree's Hippocampus or in her signifying logic, sharp as steel? In the paper of this story, in the ink that has, in part, disappeared? In the atmosphere, much as wind passes, dreams? I've tangled myself in *méconnaissance*. The un-hinged. Copernicus sat down and wept.

**THESIS:** When you meet *Mesiach*, do so via backdoors and blockades, blackmoore and brocade. Dress up and dress down. Approach with reverence, difference. Enunciate his doxa with care in the fold of your truthful stare. There at the conference where you will be asked to show your best chops aren't bacon, be asked to show your chicken neck. Are you following? The law and heuristic methods. Material and immaterial, sub-atomic and cosmic, a principle of salvation spreading like an infestation across the Judean hills, that's messianic as the law of salvation. Apples fall. Rum running during American prohibition saves us from hell. The flapjack, a Lenten desire straight out of the Roman kitchen. Apple pie, anyone?

**THESIS:** "No," he said. "There should be a law against this." What is 'this'? Turning and returning, I approach my PhD defence as I would a high school dance: dressed and afraid. What happened? "We do not know," says history. Sun sounding through the hallways of institutional memory that accumulates years of colonized trauma, convinced that light's finger speaks. "What happened," said the analysand? "Who knows," replied the analyst. Betty cracks the sun of her dress. "Dance alone," they said.

**THESIS:** The law of light, of atomic life, of keeping quiet in the library. Maybe the latter is just a bylaw… Mosaic Laws about coveting other people's things, like 'women' or the law of food requiring two kitchens. Unspoken laws of settler dominance using legalese. In Canada, there are so many laws: there are laws that keep us from colliding on the streets, and then the law that identifies citizens. One law for first nations, and another law for the rest of us.

**THESIS:** I am pretty good at spinning the laundry in with the dishes and throwing nothing out. Foolish words that might have got caught in the gears. The Golden Ass on stage who is really a nice young thing. Betty fell into the grave she had dug. She noticed the bones of Greek. She thought about her life in Tkaronto, a city her mother adopted after leaving Ottawa. In this nation called Canada. I have been mixing Cree with Greek. Miigwetch.

# NACHTRAGLICHKEIT #2 - FASTER

*"Much food stored in a cool cave"*

Lake of ice on your head.

Not all goes around
the lake. How sharp the sky, cutting
so the eyes rimmed
all the way around my face.

Katabasis is blind a cliff, Deep into Tiresias... Blind as the
wide ploughed field. Wide as a trough, the face of it going
nowhere.

Shimmer in the bowl of Eden's aleph of my heart, artichokes
and clover. Salad again. Swimming in her rough winter. "I
did them myself," she said; they tasted alright. All by myself.

She breaks winter on critical thought. Letting go. There go
her lips and anus and ears and eyes. Here comes the light,
the hidden, second hidden, inner, not between her legs or
fingers on the object cause, but deep deep down between
these very lips.

"I'll drive," she said. "Stop," we cried. The deer missed. How good it feels, this salvaged edge.

She asked me "do you believe in the universal?" I was politic and wore white. Pied-faced, 'al mode' (not *a la*). The firing squad lined up and lined out, trout in my abdomen a bulletproof belt, netting the atmosphere. Late camera's olive. Cheese.

Deep deep deep down between these lids and lips, rising. Swim, Copernicus, swim faster. Kepler is coming.

Rosenzweig starts with Falling in. If what happened was anything like anything she could have imagined, then... A grain of sound, a star you answer. Will you?

History claims there is only one.

The rim of that room, windows circling questions thin as Greek which renders History.

Witnesses to hang on the spectrum of probabilities. History's fiction flows and we know that because she talks to us.

Can you hear it, how well history remembers 'nothing'?

Oh Clorinda—I've tangled myself in *méconnaissance*. Copernicus wept.

Betty breaks winter and changes the order of things. She breaks law and can't put it together again. I'm betting that the coffee was illegal.

*Mesiach* spreading like an infestation during American prohibition. Hell of the Roman kitchen. Apple pie, anyone?

"No," he said. Sun sounding through the institutional trauma, convinced that light's finger speaks. What happened? Betty cracked her dress on aged.

One law for first nations, and another law for 'us' settlers.

From life to death to life again, Betty said. "Obviously, this hurts me more than you," said the fork to the floor.

Dull ash of katabasis.

What happened?

Nothing happened. That's the thing.

# NACHTRAGLICHKEIT #3 — EVEN FASTER

You don't know how good it feels to

SALVAGE

since

VENI VIDI VICI

you

SHALLOW DAUGHTERS

don't

START AT THE TOWER AND TURN LEFT

no

SETTLE THE BILL

because

SELAH

the truth is

THE STORES ARE SHUTTERED FOR SIESTA

hour

CAN YOU HEAR ME NOW?

I said

I WISH YOU WERE HERE

# PAS (IMPASSE)

1. *passage a l'act*
2. Passing
3. Pass muster
4. Pass.
5. *passeggiate*
6. Passé
7. Pass-key
8. Passage
9. impasse

# NACHTRAGLICHKEIT #4 -
# FASTEST

NO, he said.

The hole you carry everywhere you go, Linus.

He said no and did not say what he meant.

Many exchanges of holes in the meantime.

The question of fail.　　`

Epic fail.

Pass me in the halls and jump high.

Pass me the salt, I am sick in the heart.

I passed.

I passed through the gates and they shut behind me.

99, help me out. I am not Smart, but I get it.

This too will pass and other depressions.　　　　　　　.

I am hubris, folded into letters no one will open.

The Ph., and D. bonding all Agamben's witnesses to Badiou's event.

The assault of Cunegonde in the Lisbon streets.

The archive relies on eternity: there will always be time to find what has been

　　　discarded.

Eternity of the cat's life, or 9 of them, one in me.

Deep deep down between openings and departures, letters, numbers.

Everyone, plus one.

*Anche, mille e tre.*

Anus, ears and mouth through which I catch birds passing.

Eat it, the rim of your shambles.

Ha, deep so very deep beneath the folds of my ache,

I hear your birds singing tiny holes in the night.

My sweet, dream me all over.

# ACNOWLEDGEMENTS

This was one of those projects that was a joy to write, primarly because I did not have the academic hounds at my back, telling me what I could and couldn't do.

In this project, I wrote through what I read and I read a lot of theory by Derrida, Lacan, Zizek and Badiou, Benjamin, Balibar, Spivak, Rosenzweig... I could go on. Whether these theoriests care or not, I am indebted to them for my words.

I listened to the scholars I had as teachers and the scholars who were my mentors, and the complaints and lamentations of my colleagues, and wrote what I heard. For this collegial sharing, I am deeply grateful.

I have two primary readers for whom I offer my greatest and deepest thanks, Shane Neilson and Jim Johnstone. Shane has edited several projects of mine, and even published a poem of this MS. in *Hamilton Arts and Literature* in 2019. As an editor, Shane encouraged me to stop feeling ashamed for who I am and how it inspires what I write. As a reader of earlier drafts of this MS., and as one who encouraged me to explore the hybrid of poetry and memoir in this MS,, Shane has my deepest and sincerest thanks.

Jim Johnstone read the first draft of this project, back when it was just an ugly duckling of a poetry collection. It haunted him, he said. His interest is what lead me to send the new version, the one I built based on Shane's suggestion. Jim read this newer version and offered to publish it. For his instinct in catching my meaning in earlier drafts, and for the clarity of his eye and ear, the deft touch of his editing hand, the giving and caring responses to my ideas, I am so deeply deeply grateful.

I thank all my readers of various drafts and parts of drafts of this project, the first reader being the editor at *The Capilano Review* who published a portion of this MS. For all the readers of all the pieces I have submitted in consideration for publication and which were accepted and not, I also give thanks.

Thanks go to my friends and my neighbours, including Everet, for being solid and real in my life.

Eternal thanks to my family, without whom, as the saying goes, none of this would be possible. And for putting up with me and my creative ways, I am so extremely grateful.

Many thanks to the Ontario Arts Council and their Recommenders Grants which I received for this project.

With much love to all readers for witnessing my version of this unexpectedly unstable period in academic history.

Concetta Principe is an award-winning poet and a scholar. Her most recent book is *Stars Need Counting: Essays on Suicide*, published by Gordon Hill Press in 2021. Her first poetry collection, *Interference* (Guernica Editions, 1999), won the Bressani Award for poetry in 2000, and *This Real*, published by Pedlar Press, was long-listed for the Raymond Souster Award in 2017. She teaches at Trent University.